The Enchanted Journey:
Finding the Key That Unlocks You

Relieve Stress and Discover Keys
To the Buried Treasure of Joy Within

Terry Segal, Ph.D.

ThomasMax

Your Publisher
For The 21st Century

Acknowledgments

There are many Queens, Kings, Princesses, Princes, Journey Guides and Court Jesters to thank along my path to The Land of Enchantment.

First, I am grateful to my family of origin. My parents, Jeanne and Leo Margoluis, taught me that any dream could be built with love as its foundation. To my loving and supportive siblings, Lynne Viacava and Renny Margoluis, I thank you.

To Fred, my husband, soul mate, and Knight-in-shining-armor, thank you for being my loving and patient mid-wife while I birthed *The Enchanted Journey.*

And to our children, Sascha, Jordan, and Sage, I offer my love, always and forever, with gratitude for being my most profound teachers. Sascha, I thank you and the angels each day, for the gift of Hunter. He is enchantment personified.

Thanks to my, not "oldest" but "longest-time" childhood friends, Cathy Tesserot and Steven Jay, for thinking that everything I do is wonderful.

Dear friends, Dr. David and Monika Eichler, thank you for adding your brilliance and compassion to my life and for helping me battle the Dragons of Doubt when they breathed fire on my neck.

Ruth Eichler, I thank you for your patient and loving guidance.

Dr. Susan Russell, my "sisterfriend" and colleague, I offer gratitude for plugging me into the circuitry of Greenwich University and for remaining as a beacon of light.

To Anna-Claire and Matthew Myers, thanks for your humor and sensitivity.

With deepest appreciation, I acknowledge Dr. Thomas McMurrain and Dr. Marsha Kaufman McMurrain for believing in this project and for providing a forum in which to test-drive it.

David Zebrowitz, my technology wizard, without you, my words would still be stuck inside of the computer.

I give thanks to the memory of my dear friends, both talented writers, Dr. Jaqueline P. Rector and Dagmar Marshall, who will always be an inspiration. I hear you cheering among the angels.

I thankfully acknowledge the students and professors who participated in the formal study for their time and enthusiasm. To Dr. Robert E. Nunley, Dr. Ann P. Nunley, and Dr. Bernard O. Williams, I appreciate your support and intuitive insights.

To Dr. C. Norman Shealy, I am grateful, beyond measure, for your spirit and passion that provide others with a vehicle to transport dreams into reality.

Many thanks to my Barnes & Noble critique group and North Point Writers. You've been gentle, honest and encouraging, always. In alphabetical order, so there is no quibbling over favorites, you are: Mark All, Terry Baddoo, Kelly Bell, Buzz Bernard, Cecilia Branhut, Michael Buchanan, Paul A. Bussard, Tammy Dahlgren, Rob Elliott, Ann Foskey, Robert Gilbreath, Dr. John Sheffield, Marre Stevens, John Tabellione, Pat Thurmond, George Weinstein and John Witkowski.

Hugs and appreciation to my friend and gentle reader, Terri DelCampo.

Special thanks to Lee Clevenger at ThomasMax Publishing for understanding the heart of a writer and for clearing the weeds from my path.

And finally, gratitude to the Divine Source, and to angels, both incarnate and disincarnate, who assist me daily. This could not have been completed without the presence of all of you.

Contents

About the Author

Terry Segal earned her Ph.D. in Energy Medicine from Greenwich University, Australia, while attending a sister University in the United States. She has a Master of Arts Degree in Educational Psychology from California State University at Northridge, as well as a Master of Arts Degree in Theatre from the University of Miami, in Florida.

A licensed Marriage and Family Therapist, in both Georgia and California, Dr. Segal maintains a private practice in Georgia. Through her experience as a therapist for the last quarter of a century, she believes that healing and growth occur as blocks are removed, and balance is restored on the physical, mental, spiritual and emotional planes. She specializes in Hypnotherapy, Energy Anatomy and the arts, as tools for assessment and healing. Humor and imagination play a vital role in her work.

As a member of North Point Writers, the author's poetry and prose have been published in an anthology titled: *North Point of View: Tales of Alpharetta and Beyond.* Her work was also selected for inclusion in two volumes of *O, Georgia! A Collection of Georgia's Newest and Most Promising Writers.* She is a long-time member of the Atlanta Writers Club.

Dr. Segal is the creator and facilitator of the experiential workshop entitled: ***The Enchanted Journey: Finding the Key That Unlocks You.*** She has been a contributing editor for various parenting, health and beauty publications. Additionally, she is a mixed-media artist and dancer.

Contact Dr. Segal online at www.DrTerrySegal.com.

This book is dedicated to my husband and best friend, Fred, my children, Sascha, Jordan and Sage, and to my grandson, Hunter.

I love you, always and forever.

May The Enchanted Journey *be a source of Tikkun Olam; repair of the world.*

Foreword

Life should be fun and, well "enchanting." If it is not, you are suffering from the miasma of society—depression. Freud, one of history's more unhappy souls, stated that most people have a death wish. Freud, of course, was addicted to cocaine! Eric Berne stated that we all have a life script, which we set in early life to end at a certain age of a specific disease. He reported that his life script called for him to die at age 60 of a heart attack. And he did.

John Knowles, late President of the Rockefeller Foundation, stated that 85% of illness is the result of an unhealthy lifestyle. Today at least 29% of adults still smoke; a third are just plain obese and another third are overweight. Many more are couch potatoes, spending forty hours in front of the television, eating abdominally, and popping all too many drugs, many illicit street drugs, plus an excess of alcohol. Most are depressed. None of this sounds enchanting. No wonder there is an existential crisis.

If we look at history, the situation has changed little over the past two thousand years. A majority of individuals have lived unsatisfying lives. And yet, a few, at all times, have experienced the essence of living a full, joyous, enchanting life. In the past 50 years, the fields of Transpersonal Psychology and Humanistic Psychology have opened the doors to the concepts of becoming self-actualized, spiritually awakened humans. *The Enchanted Journey* takes you not only through the open doors but guides you in practical experiences, which are fun and mind/spirit expanding. The fact that you have opened this book proves that you are interested in expanding your conscious realization of the potential of life. The journey is well worth your time and energy. This is a book not just for reading but also for DOING and BEING. This is the beginning of one of the most important journeys of your life---the journey to explore, enrich and optimize your potential. The human potential is one of great joy, exuberance, Enlightenment. The true spiritual journey is that to rediscover your connection with the real you---soul/spirit—indeed your inseparable core, the divine within. Mystics, artists, poets, and some novelists have described the result of The Enchanted Journey. Now you can follow the simple and fun path yourself. It is the "Road Less Traveled" but it is a road well worth your time and energy. Welcome to the Real Journey of Life.

C. Norman Shealy, M.D., Ph.D.
President, Holos University Graduate Seminary
Founding President, American Holistic Medical Association

Introduction

This manual is a map, designed to help you maneuver through the enchanted journey of your life. It contains anecdotes, case histories, and exercises that you can apply to your own life, in order to reduce stress and create enchantment.

Many of us were taught not to write in books, but provided that you own this book and are not checking it out of a library, reading it in a bookstore, or borrowing it from a friend, feel free to scribble notes or doodle in the margins. That can make your journey more memorable and meaningful for you.

When I studied abnormal psychology, in the margins of my book, I jotted down the names of people I know that could qualify for each diagnosis. Sometimes I drew pictures of them. (By the way, if you're a relative, don't bother rummaging through my library—I used pencil and erased everything upon the conferring of my degree.) For the written exercises in this book, instead of the margins, I suggest writing on separate paper. That way, you can do the exercises again and again, without being swayed by where you were on the path, previously.

Embarking on *The Enchanted Journey* is a lifetime adventure. I'm on it with you. You're not alone. Occasionally, I still get off-balance and the dragons breathe fire down my neck. But when they do, I reach for the Enchanted Keys. There's a set waiting for you. More than one key may actually fit into a lock. When it's the right key, its perfect alignment of notches and grooves will allow it to turn easily and open the doors to possibilities you never knew existed.

Right now, **YOU ARE HERE.**

What's possible is for you to reach **ENCHANTMENT** (a more balanced and joyful life**.)**

When you've completed the journey, you will have earned your set of Enchanted Keys and learned how to tackle the following tasks:

- To target stressful areas in your life.
  - A. In the mind: To become aware of the internalized Dragons, in all of their forms, and of your Guides who will help you validate yourself, so you may choose your thoughts and actions well.
  - B. In the emotions and body: To notice your body's feelings, signals and ways in which thoughts affect you.
- To become mindful.
- To change your perception of stress.
- To manage or eliminate stress through coping strategies that incorporate joyful activities.
- To use journaling for the purpose of self-exploration and stress reduction.
- To heighten the awareness of sensory experiences that help to create enchantment.
- To experience enchantment through reconnection with the purity, playfulness and joyfulness of the spirited child within each of us.
- To pinpoint areas of clutter as they exist on the physical, emotional, mental and spiritual planes.
- To explore your personal style of humor.
- To use movement to enhance productivity, relieve stress from the physical body, and aid organs in their ability to function to their optimum capacity.
- To combine shapes, colors, textures, and images, to create a journal without words. (art)
- To realign with nature. To find an internal "place of peace" from which to release stress and experience relaxation. (meditation)

May you enjoy *The Enchanted Journey* and find the key that unlocks you.

The Birth of The Enchanted Journey Tour

I writhed. I shrieked. I pushed, until the blood vessels burst in my eyeballs. I was birthing *The Enchanted Journey*. Fortunately for others, this all took place in my head, as I was attending a continuing education lecture at the time.

It had been difficult to concentrate on the droning voice of the lecturer who presented information that could neither be applied to my personal life nor my psychotherapy practice. I was also squeezed into a metal chair, in a sea of chairs filled with the bodies of other therapists, psychologists, and nurses. We neared license-renewal time and took our bitter pills by sitting for hours in a crowded conference room that alternated in temperature between Antarctic meat-locker and Haitian sun deck. Six hours to be exact. After realizing I had looked at my watch 137 times in the first half hour, I knew I'd have to do something to stay awake and to keep from actually screaming aloud.

I decided to mentally journey to the beach. I closed my eyes and heard the song of the seagulls in the distance. I felt the mist of the ocean on my cheek. I drew in a deep and cleansing breath—the harsh realization entering my nostrils—that the attendee to my right was a smoker.

Augh. I popped my eyes open and met his bloodshot stare. He shouldn't have worn his tweed jacket to the beach but he did, and it felt scratchy against my arm. It, too, held the smoky remnants of his habit. "Ohhh, what if it weren't ocean spray and he had spit on me while whispering to someone seated near me?" I forced myself back to my blanket on the beach.

I snuggled into my chair and slid my insteps under the grains of warm, golden sand. I'd journal while sipping my peach tea. No, make that raspberry tea. I fantasized about the kind of workshop I wished I were attending. During it, time passed quickly. Ideas were introduced that were useful to me, both personally and professionally. It was fun and I wore comfortable clothes. I had space and could even move around the room if I wanted. I was invited to draw, dream, listen to music, write about things that matter to me, and laugh. How enchanting. *The Enchanted Journey* morphed into a gift I wanted to give to my tired, stressed-out colleagues and to myself.

Two weeks later, I brainstormed with my friend, Tom McMurrain, at a local coffee house. He has a Ph.D. in psychology and well understood the hellish nightmare that obtaining CEUs can sometimes be. I shared my vision with him and excitedly scribbled ideas on a napkin. Two months later, I presented *The Enchanted Journey* workshop at the Georgia World Congress Center for 350 pre-school teachers from all over the state. Tom's wife, Marsha Kaufman McMurrain, a Ph.D. in early childhood education, had been put in charge of finding a guest speaker to talk to these teachers about stress reduction. The Universe clearly gave a green light to my daydreams. I received the most wonderful feedback from attendees and continued to present the workshop to others.

I offered it at various locations, for both large and small groups. I created a ninety-minute version, a two-and-a-half hour version, and the six hour version. Once, I did the entire six-hour workshop for just one person. No, it wasn't my mother. Several people had registered, but due to a flu epidemic and poor weather conditions, only one person attended. It was too close to the deadline for the submission of continuing education units and she needed them to renew her license. I couldn't turn her away. It proved to be a learning experience for me, as well. She was a very nice woman but in offering a six-hour lecture to one person, I was forced to practice every single idea that I preach, just to get through the day.

Fast-forward two years to the first day of my doctoral program in Energy Medicine, through Greenwich University. That's located on Norfolk Island, in Australia. I, however, was attending classes on location in the United States, at Dr. C. Norman Shealy's farm in the Midwest.

David Eichler, an apparition in the dirt parking lot who, thankfully, turned out to be a real person, offered me a ride. He, another doctoral student at Greenwich, and the University of Kansas as well, offered to become my personal chauffeur. He and I, and later his wife, Monika, became fast friends.

Dr. Shealy welcomed the small group of us and we spent the next four days, eight hours a day, firming up the details of the topic of our doctoral dissertations. It was hard to believe. It was akin to being fitted for a cap and gown, and practicing commencement exercises on the first day of school.

We were told by Dr. Shealy that it would be a tough road. He let us know that our task was to bring scientific research and credibility to the field of Energy Medicine. That conscious awareness of the integration of science and spirit would have to be held in every breath. Hey, no pressure there! No stress. Above everything else, he said that we must have passion for our chosen focus of study.

I immediately had fifteen topics in mind. I postulated that people with Obsessive Compulsive Disorder (OCD) had been responsible for tragic events in their past lives, had karmic carryovers of hyper-vigilance in their current ones, and could be cleared through Past-Life Regression Hypnotherapy. All right. I was asked what else I had. I was prepared to explore the correlation between a child's birth experience and the subsequent development of his or her personality. Dr. Shealy and the group of students patiently listened to all of my ideas. Dr. Shealy said they were interesting, but that I lacked the passion for them that was required. I was being "too cerebral, not enough heart." Feedback I had never received in my life. I was confused. I thought I *had* to check my heart at the door in order to proceed with my Ph.D., a.k.a., "Pile it higher and Deeper" program.

I was trying to remember how to breathe when David rescued me, again. He asked if he could present his ideas. I knew he was graciously offering me time to regroup. He spoke excitedly about the examination of a subtle energy transduction device that he wanted to test on the anxiety levels of students in a public school setting.

In that moment, I decided that I was an idiot, and had no business being there. "Terry, I'd like to return to you. Have you decided on a topic?" Dr. Shealy's voice was kind, but he awaited an answer. His face blurred in my vision when a huge flood of salty water took over my tear ducts. My vocal chords tensed, producing a sound similar to a creaking rocking chair. My sweat glands, having no plans elsewhere, opened like rodeo gates and an Elvis snarl inhabited my upper lip as it quivered. I don't think you're supposed to cry uncontrollably in front of your mentor and fellow doctoral students on the first day of school. But I did.

We were offered a fifteen-minute dignity break. Other people simply used it to pee or stretch. Nearly everyone else had his or her topic decided. I was in a room full of other overachievers, who were achieving, while I was behaving like a blithering fool.

A few students I'd never met hugged me. I was hosting a full-on pity party when one of them asked what I do for my day job. I told her about my practice and *The Enchanted Journey*. Dr. Shealy sprinted across the room toward me. "Whatever you're speaking about," he said, "that's it! That's how you should look when you're talking about your focus of study." Thank goodness I hadn't been discussing having sex with my husband.

The Enchanted Journey would become my focus of study. Who knew? And who knew that this book would be written as a result of Dr. Shealy's inspiration and that of my friends and colleagues? They helped me realize my role as an Enchantress and my dedication to assisting you in the discovery of your joy, your peace, your humor, and your inner light. I had to take the first steps in order to clear the path. Now I'm ready to lead you.

Let's embark on the journey.

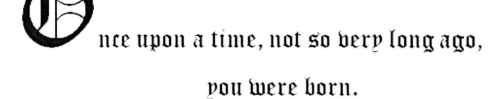

Once upon a time, not so very long ago,

you were born.

You were all about love, joy, and sharing.
A bundle of energy waiting to unfold.

You saw your first butterfly,

felt sand in your toes

or snow on your nose.

You noticed the smallest of bugs.

🐜......

You took notes on the beauty of the world and tucked

them into your secret heart.

You danced like the wind, sang like a bird, and

borrowed God's palette to paint the sky.

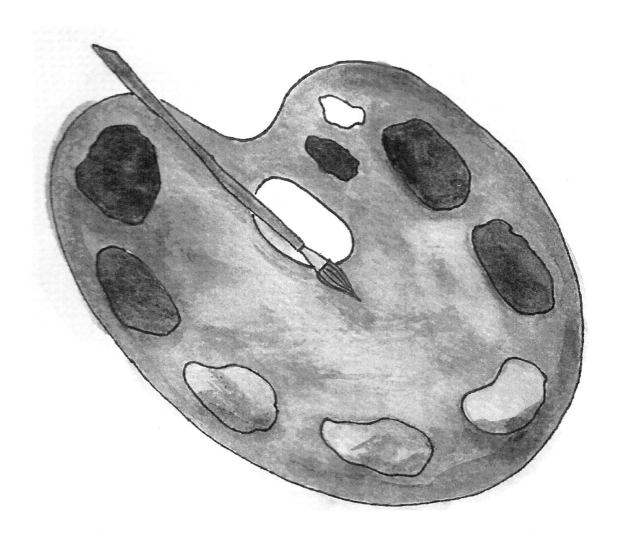

𝕻ou were the 𝕼ueen or 𝕶ing of the castles you made.

But then one day you discovered there were

DRAGONS.

You quickly put a lock on your secret heart,

and sent your soul away to the dungeon.

You breathed a promise to unearth it

Someday.

But it was so buried; YOU forgot it was there.

Until one day, you caught a glimpse of a memory.

It was of your face, with a smile.

Then there was more.

Your voice, laughing.

Your light, which had lit your path. You, moving any

which way, unrestricted.

You, feeling love in your heart.

And you remembered...

...all, but where you put the key.

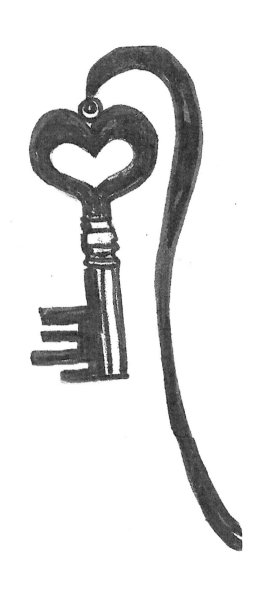

Let me guide you on a journey, gently back,

to the joy,

the Dragons,

and the key

that holds the secret

to the treasures and magic that are

YOU.

ʗ

(not) The End.

Just the Beginning...

The Map and Map Key

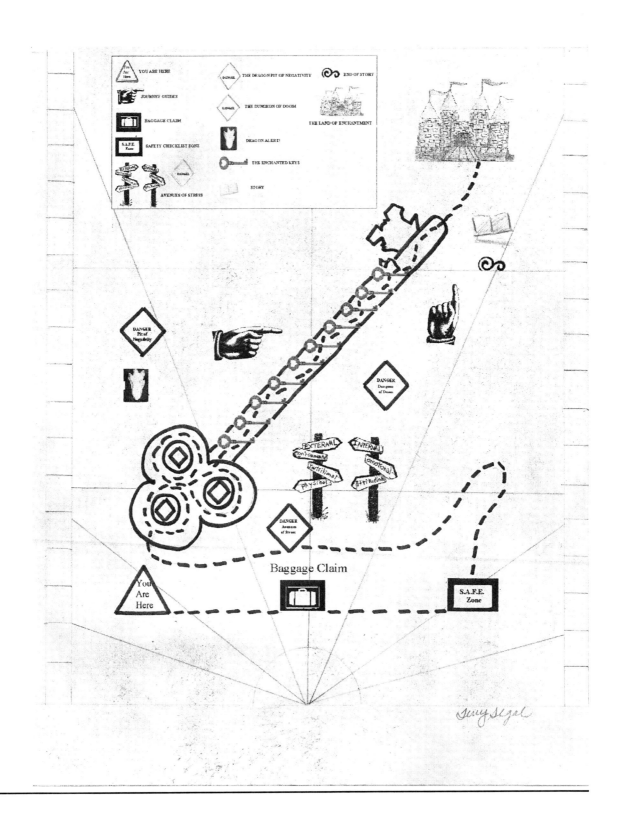

Chapter One: The Map Key Defined

Points of Interest

JOURNEY GUIDES

BAGGAGE CLAIM

SAFETY CHECKLIST ZONE

DRAGON PIT OF NEGATIVITY

DUNGEON OF DOOM

   **THE ENCHANTED KEYS**

   **STORY**

   **END OF STORY**

What You Need

Please keep an open mind and the will to change at least one thing in your life.
Also bring along a composition book, journal, or some blank sheets of paper and a writing utensil, to record your experiences. You'll be required to learn two new languages: one is the language of the Critical Dragon. It's an ancient language and you may already speak it without awareness. You must learn to recognize it so that you will no longer use it or fall under the spell of others who do. The second language is that of Enchantment. It's one of the original romance languages.

<u>Chapter Two: The Journey Begins</u>

Points of Interest

YOU ARE HERE

There's no turning back. Chances are that you're stressed, tired, and looking for answers. You've come to the right place. Your goal is to reach **ENCHANTMENT**: a stress-free perspective on life that results in rich sensory experiences.

This is a strategy that, if played well, offers great reward. You may encounter unexpected events along the way. Some may be awe-inspiring while others, quite challenging.

Time to take inventory of everything you've brought with you to the **YOU ARE HERE** spot. Yeah, other people may have driven you here, dragged you by your hair, you may have rolled your eyes and come on your own-- yatta yatta. The point is that **YOU ARE HERE** and not sipping tropical smoothies in the land of **ENCHANTMENT**…yet.

So, how did you get here?

Let's frisk your spirit and see. Is your desire to improve the quality of your life prompted by others or is it truly *your* desire? No one else can make you happy or skinny, so if you wish for change, roll up your sleeves and let's continue.

Empty your pockets to ensure you're free of weapons that can sabotage a good time. Any doubting thoughts in there? Any old tapes ready to be replayed for the four thousandth time? Let's be sure that you're not carrying food that can fuel the fire of your dragons. Stress, as well as toxic thoughts, feelings, and behaviors, are yummy treats that feed those dragons.

JOURNEY GUIDES

Allow me to introduce myself. I'm **The Enchantress** and will be here with you for the entire journey. I'll point out your wounded feelings, give you a hug with hot chocolate when you need it, and offer balance. I'll assist you with recognizing your Internal Enchantress, or Sorcerer, who can see you, hear you, validate your self-esteem (maybe even your parking), while offering options for your next move.

I'll also introduce you to the staff as they appear. Many of the **Journey Guides** hang out at the Avenues of Stress because it's such an important gathering place. They'll speak to you about stress and its negative effects. Some will use the terms stress and anxiety interchangeably. Stress and anxiety are to the body what pollution is to the environment. There are many more Journey Guides for your discovery. **The Kings, Queens, Princes, Princesses, Knights in Shining Armor, Alchemists, Magicians and Wizards** will appear in various forms to impart their wisdom. You may already move among them, find that you're related to them, read books written by them, or give birth to them. Those who will join us here are the ones who have crossed my path on my own Enchanted Journey. They are all teachers. Please pay close attention.

BAGGAGE CLAIM

This is the checkpoint for discovering just how heavy and oversized your baggage in life is. It highlights all of the ways in which you create, experience, and share your stress with others, while lugging it around in your body, mind, spirit, and emotions.

You need to fess up about how much stress you're lugging on board right now and also how much you've let it affect you and others. Don't mess with The Enchantress. Tell the truth. To do so, you must become discerning. No more arm to forehead, throwing yourself on the ground, yelling dramatically, "I'm so stressed out!" On a scale of 1-10, how would you rate your level of stress in this moment, if ten is under more pressure than a lid on a vacuum-sealed jar of pickles, and one is like an elastic band around Twiggy's waist? Using the same scale, how would you rate your stress during the last week? The last month? Last year? This lifetime? Your past lives?

All right. Now that you've acknowledged that you actually do have baggage on board (and I'm proud of you for that) let's review the Safety Checklist so that you and others are not further burdened by your stuff.

S.A.F.E. Zone

SAFETY CHECKLIST ZONE

You will be instructed about how to stay safe when we approach The Pitfalls, which include The Dragon Pit of Negativity and The Dungeon of Doom.

Stress detector awareness

Avenues of stress

Focus on your body's stress signals

Establishment of an action to disarm the alarms

Stress Detector Awareness

These loud and obnoxious alarms will sound when you encounter what you perceive as stress. Note that these alarms are individualized. Until you learn to disarm them, be prepared to receive small shocks when the alarms are tripped. Don't worry though; you're probably already numb to them. You may have gotten so used to being stressed that it has become a natural state for you.

Avenues of Stress

When we arrive at the Avenues of Stress, you'll learn more about all the ways that you can be bombarded by stress. Critical Dragon tries to guest star in this information session but don't worry, I'm on it.

Focus on Your Body's Stress Signals

Stress is experienced differently by everyone. The source of each person's stress is as individual as he or she is. I'll give you a chance to determine your causes of stress and what works best to manage or eliminate them.

Establishment of an Action to Disarm the Alarms

You have your own methods of calming, soothing, or supporting yourself. We'll figure out which action needs to be invoked in order to restore balance.

DANGER
Pit of
Negativity

PITFALLS

The Dragon Pit of Negativity

If you fall off the path, you'll plunge into the same caverns in which I, and most other mortals, have fallen. You'll drop into the Dragon Pit of Negativity and do battle with the Dragons. You can get out. I will help you, but it's easier to catch yourself and regain your balance than it is to climb back up. There are some definite areas in which the ground is muddier, the incline steeper, and the temperature may change without warning. I'll alert you to these things until you get used to doing that for yourself. In the meantime, do try to stay aware. There might be perfectly flat, firm ground on which you slip for no apparent reason. If you stay in the pit long enough, you'll find yourself in the Dungeon of Doom.

DANGER
Dungeon
of Doom

The Dungeon of Doom

Stay away. Nothing ever changes in this dungeon. No options are explored, no dreams dreamed, and no doomed destinies altered.

You'll know when you're in the Dungeon of Doom for the first time, or have cycled around and returned to it. In it, the self-deprecating CDs that continue on Repeat-All can't be quieted; you forget that you have alternate choices and others who can help you. Rumor and research support the idea that it takes approximately twenty-one days to change a habit. Please don't stay in the dungeon during those three weeks. Extra self-care and love is required at this time.

And then there are the Dragons…

Dragon Alert

Please heed the Dragon Alerts. They will warn you that dragons approach. Through experience, I can spot them at a distance. By the end of the tour, you will too. But for now, don't venture off the path.

Beware. Learning about your dragons is only for the hardy. They can come at you externally, from all sides, or internally, through your body, thoughts, or attitudes. Often, you won't be aware that they inhabit your space. Learn to recognize them so that you can call them by name and transform them. (I'll teach you how.)

Don't lose your balance. The pit is teeming with dragons. They squash the spirit and squelch enchantment. They are trash-talkers who rob you of your self-esteem. Do not, I repeat, *do not* attempt to slay these dragons. Summon The Enchantress (call me, we'll do lunch) and the other Journey Guides if you feel threatened. Remember not to feed the dragons.

Dragons are the type to tip-toe up behind you and, just when you think you might have heard something, blow a party horn in your ear. Sometimes they dress up like someone you love, to confuse you. Other times, like in the soap operas on TV, they whisper to you to make you think you're crazy. You're probably not. You need to be on to their tricks, shine the search light on them, and befriend them. Dragons can be helpful to have around when you need them. They just can't be allowed to run the show. Because your dragon awareness is so important to your health and well-being, in a bit, I'll take you through a hands-on trip into the dragon pit.

THE ENCHANTED KEYS

The Enchanted Keys will unlock the doors that return you to the path. Keep them with you at all times. There are ten stops at which you will have the opportunity to be granted a key. Each opens a different lock. These keys represent the tools you'll use in the world, after you complete the guided tour and embark on a journey of your own. Every key has a name and will be given to you in this order: **MINDFULNESS, ALTERED PERCEPTIONS, JOURNALING, SENSORY EXPERIENCES, REDUCED CLUTTER, HUMOR, MOVEMENT, ART, NATURE, AND MEDITATION.** You may use them individually or in combination with one another to progress on the path.

STORY

Many stories will be shared with you during the journey. This storybook signals each of them. (Don't you hate it when you want to tell someone about something you read and can't find it again? Problem solved.)

 **END OF STORY**

This scroll symbol marks the end of a story.

DISCLAIMER

Of course, it's your choice to stay in the pit or the dungeon and continue to live among the dragons because they're familiar. But bear in mind that, on the other side of the pit, enchantment awaits you. There is no key that allows control of the events themselves, just your response to them.

I dare you to choose **ENCHANTMENT**...

Chapter Three: Stress

Please consider what the word, "stress" means to you. What does it evoke? Take out your journal and jot down your definition of stress and what being stressed feels like for you.

If you're reading ahead here and didn't stop to write down your definition and experience of stress then I have to yell at you. Not really. Enchantresses don't yell. What that suggests, though, is that you're trying to race through the journey and that's not enchanting.

If you did write it down, group hug.

S.A.F.E.

Stress Detector Awareness

Stress means many different things to people and manifests in different ways. It can wear various disguises and tension is a big one. Perhaps you're walking around with constricted muscles, restricted breathing, frequent headaches, cramped stomach, curled fingers and toes or furrowed eyebrows, thinking that this is normal.

Understand that each of you has your own Stress Detector System and what triggers the alarms in one of you does not necessarily trigger them in another (even if that other person loves you.) Sometimes we can feel judged if we're stressed by something and another person, especially a loved one, trivializes our response or worse, thinks it's silly or unfounded.

   **JOURNEY GUIDE**

One of our first Journey Guides has been spotted. He's Dr. Hans Selye.[1] Let's see what wisdom he has for us.

Hans Selye
Pioneer in the field of stress and illness who studied injured animals or those placed under extreme conditions. He determined that distress turns into disease.

Not only was Selye the man who coined the term "stress," but it was as recently as the 1950s. (Tell me that isn't riveting party-chat.) The good news is that if you were born before then, you didn't know you were stressed. You just thought you were tired. Guess what else? If you continue to ignore your alarms of distress, they're likely to get louder until they've gotten your attention by making you sick.

Selye not only defined stress as a response to a stimulus or event, but also differentiated the stress from the cause of the stress and named that "the stressor." This is not an invitation to rename your mother-in-law, but simply a tool for distinguishing the difference between a stressor and a stress response.

The stressor is the external demand put on you, whereas stress is your individualized response to your internal experience of that stressor.

Look behind you. If a dragon is chasing you, the dragon is the stressor. If you're gasping, running, sweating, or screaming, that is your stress response to the stressor.

In an effort to resist or meet these external demands, Selye discovered that we might get defensive or exhibit a variety of other strategies to help us cope with these pressures.

The term strain refers to the deterioration that occurs over time from the resistance to adaptation or change. Selye also discovered that it doesn't matter if the strain is caused by eustress (perceived positive stress, if you can imagine such a thing), like the birth of a child, an anticipated move or promotion, or distress (perceived negative stress), such as death, loss of job or divorce. What does matter is how intensely we experience the demand for adaptation or change.

Seyle even came up with GAS. Now, now, GAS stands for General Adaptation Syndrome. His research showed that bodies, as survival mechanisms, adapt to the stress they're exposed to repeatedly. But then, as you're well aware of, these bodies just can't take it any more and they collapse, get diseases, or become out of balance in some other way.

It's vital to recognize the demands put upon you and your ability to cope with them. You can't control whether or not a dragon charges at you, but you can alter your own experience of it afterward, and sometimes during it, if you can learn to disarm the alarms.

From this point forward, you're required to refer to your safety checklist when a stress detector sounds. Remember that just because you may have spent years numbing yourself to these alarms doesn't mean that they're not still blaring. Your mission (yes, you have a choice about whether or not to accept it) is to do things differently than you've ever done them.

Two journeymen are passing us on the path. They're the research team of psychologists, Drs. Richard S. Lazarus and Raymund A. Launier. [2]

JOURNEY GUIDES

Lazarus and Launier
They focused on the connection between the demands put upon each of us and our own ability to deal with them without harmful results.

Slightly different from Selye's view, theirs is that stress isn't necessarily caused by an environmental stimulus, due to a particular aspect of a person, or simply a response. They're all about the individual's ability to deal with things and remain in a healthful state.

Imagine an animal lover who has grown up around dogs. He or she may see a dog, experience delight, and move to greet it. Someone else, who has had a traumatic experience with a dog, may view the dog as a stressor, the same as if it were a dragon, and run in fear. So, in this example, the dog lover would have no demands put upon him or her to cope, whereas, the other person would have to overcome a great deal of stress to manage his or her response.

What one person may consider stressful on an external or internal level, another person may not. Someone may perceive an event as stressful on one occasion, but not on another. As a person's emotional or physical state fluctuates, so may his or her perception of whether or not an event is stressful.

One of the problems of everyday life is that alarms continually sound and we often forget that we're in charge of turning them off. Some people never turn theirs off. Reprogram your internal codes so that your alarms don't trip at the same intensity whether the stressor is the plummeting elevator you're trapped in, or the chocolate milk your child spilled on the rug. You may discover that you repeatedly trot down the same Avenues of Stress that made you so tense in the first place.

Let's go on a tour of these Avenues of Stress. Once familiar with them, you'll be more likely to recognize when you're going the wrong way and choose differently.

 **Dragon Alert!**

Wow. I just barely had a chance to warn you that a dragon approached. It was going to try to convince you that you don't need information about stress. See how sneaky they can be? Keep moving.

As part of your stress detector awareness training you need to learn about the different avenues so that when you veer off the path you can return. Be careful that you don't get led into a dead end...literally. Take a deep breath, exhale, and I'll help you navigate your way.

Avenues of Stress

These avenues can help you identify what kind of stress you're experiencing; whether it's external, environmental, nutritional, physical, internal, emotional or attitudinal. (And you thought that stress was just stress.)

In scientific literature, stress is described in three distinct ways.

First, an event or environmental stimulus that creates tension or arousal in a person is considered to be an *external* stress, occurring outside of the body and includes environmental, nutritional, and physical stress.

Secondly, *internal* stress refers to the mental state of tension or arousal that occurs inside of a person and consists of emotional and attitudinal stress.

The third way that stress may be experienced is in the *physical reaction* of the body.

EXTERNAL STRESS

Environmental stress: As the name implies, these are stressors that come from the environment. They may include exposure to chemicals or pesticides present in your food, home, fields, and in the air you breathe. You might be exposed, daily, to cleaners in offices and restaurants, or pesticides used on school or campus lawns. Exhaust from cars can contribute to your level of environmental stress, as do cluttered work spaces or living conditions. Your dragons fill take-out cartons with hostility from other frustrated, stressed people and feed them to you when you're not paying attention. The next thing you know, instead of hearing the music of your life, all you're taking in is annoying static that you can't turn off. (But you can.)

Nutritional stress: This is the effect on your physical body of what you put into it. Remember the expression, "Garbage in, garbage out?" Nutritional stress, which begins with the choices you make, can result from eating poor quality food that is processed or chemically altered, eating excessive amounts of food, or not enough, eating at times of the day that your body should be engaged in processes other than digestion, or by depriving it of the water it needs to stay hydrated.

Foods that normally don't bother you can send your system off-kilter if they're prepared in an unhealthy way, eaten in combination with other foods, or ingested when your system is compromised for various reasons. Instead of water, you may flood your body with stimulating fluids topped with a dollop of fat. Perhaps you consume too much alcohol, fatty food, or salt, resulting in unwanted weight gain, weight loss, allergies, fatigue, or illness.

Think back to the last time you shut off a nutritional stress alarm. Jot it down. It may have been when you spoke into the clown's mouth, ordering the greasy burger you consumed on your way home from work. Perhaps it was during a walk to the refrigerator for the hot-fudge sundae that called to you at two o'clock in the morning, or maybe when you received the large-sized, extra-super-duper serving of low self-esteem you inadvertently ordered with your meal. Look across the room. Is there a dragon in the corner doing the happy dance of recognition?

It's okay. Everyone makes poor choices from time to time. Let's not repeat the ones that send you on a barge, further and further away from **ENCHANTMENT. Physical stress: The result of stress or strain that is placed on your physical body.** This can be caused from lack of sleep, imbalanced elimination of waste, or emotional challenges that take their toll on the body. Repeated physical exertion can create a stress response. You can see how one alarm can trip another. Take a moment to feel some compassion for yourself (nails on a chalkboard to dragons) and understand how you might have turned all of your alarms off when you were overwhelmed.

INTERNAL STRESS

Have you ever received news that suddenly made you feel as if you were hit in the head with a baseball bat?

"Mrs. Miller, I have your test results back. We thought you were well into menopause. What a surprise that you're pregnant!"

This kind of shock can alter your ability to think or sort out your emotions. You may behave in a way that's either passive or active and your emotions may be volatile. You might be irritable, explosive or demonstrate displaced anger. (Displaced anger is kicking the dog or screaming at your family when you're really mad at someone else.)

Psychological resistance is the "No, no, no, that can't be…" response.

If you're dealing with internal stress, the meaning you assign to your thoughts is key. Something that you'd normally find non-threatening or even funny can become intimidating or personally confrontational.

Let's say you've been feeling badly about yourself because you've gained a few pounds. It may not even be apparent to your co-workers. Normally you're known around the office for having a good sense of humor, but if you've been building internal stress over the weight gain, your reactions may surprise you, as well as others. Imagine that you bent over to pick up your pen and someone yells, "Look it's a full moon!" Typically you might laugh and throw a wadded-up piece of paper at the person who said it, but under internal stress, that joke could send you into a choke hold on the jokester's neck, or running out of the room in tears. Rational thinking and decision-making ability usually leave as well. (You would need a hug.)

Emotional and Attitudinal stress: Your *perception* of the events that occur externally or internally and your reactive response to them. As in the afore-mentioned example, you may respond with a knee-jerk reaction based on how you feel in the moment. Too often, we internalize other people's lack of sensitivity. Well guess what? We get to take a deep breath and decide how we feel about what they say.

Then our actions can follow suit. We can't control other people, just how we respond to them.

Dragons can dress up in costumes so I have to double-check that this is a Guide in our midst. Yes. Dr. Jon-Kabat-Zinn[3] comes into our awareness at this point.

JOURNEY GUIDE

Jon Kabat-Zinn

His research focuses on mind/body interactions for healing, and the clinical use of mindfulness meditation training for people with chronic pain and/or stress-related disorders.

Through the work of Kabat-Zinn, the connection between the mind and body is apparent. Kabat-Zinn suggests we separate ourselves from the content of our thoughts. So if we say, "I'm anxious," that's like waving a magic wand that turns us into the anxiety. We need separateness from the anxious thoughts and feelings through recognizing that they are there, without becoming them. We might say, instead, "I'm having anxious thoughts." Also helpful, is to perceive an interconnectedness within ourselves, others, the world, the universe, and all of nature.

Dr. Meyer Friedman[4] and Dr. Redford Williams[5] are important gentlemen who studied the detrimental effects of negative personality traits on the heart.

JOURNEY GUIDES

Meyer Friedman and Redford Williams

Friedman discovered Type-A and Type-B personalities and their connection to heart disease.
Williams focused on the component of hostility and its contribution to heart disease.

You're probably familiar with the attitudes and behaviors of Friedman's Type-A and Type-B personalities. Type-A's are characterized by their impatience, hostility and aggression. They exhibit a sense of urgency with regard to time and appear to be driven and competitive. If you've ever stood behind the Type-A's in a movie line, they're the ones who are shifting their weight, jangling the pocket coins, and running to the front of the line to pay off the first person so that they don't have to wait.

Type-B's tend to be more relaxed and easygoing. They exhibit the opposite characteristics of the Type-A personality, and also tend to be more introspective, or contemplative, in their nature. (Which one are you?)

Studies were done to determine whether or not there was a personality type that was prone to heart disease. Type-A's had developed coronary heart disease at two to four times the rate of Type-Bs.

In a later study, Williams proved that the component of hostility was a stronger predictor of heart disease than the combined patterns of the Type-A individual. So if that isn't an invitation for you Type-A's to chill the heck out and change your attitude, I don't know what is.

Dr. C. Norman Shealy[6], my mentor, and a King among men, reminds us that at least eighty-five percent of all illnesses are the result of lifestyle choices and are, therefore, avoidable.

JOURNEY GUIDE

C. Norman Shealy

One of the world's leading experts in pain management. He was among the first physicians ever to specialize in the resolution of chronic pain. He is the author of numerous books and publications on healing and is the founding President of The American Holistic Medical Association.

Shealy defines stress as the cumulative effect of the total physical, chemical and emotional pressure that we experience.

Stress and anxiety and fear, oh my! I'll explain the subtle differences, in case the dragons try to confuse you. Stress generally refers to some kind of stimulus, like fear or pain, which disturbs the normal balance of an organism.

Anxiety usually refers to a state of apprehension. Dr. Frederick "Fritz" Perls[7] explains it well.

JOURNEY GUIDE

Frederick "Fritz" Perls

The developer of the existential form of therapy called Gestalt therapy.

Perls believed that "nothing exists except the now," and described anxiety as "the gap between the now and the later." He emphasized the importance of living in the "here and now," as a way to cope with feelings of anxiety.

Everywhere we turn there are guides along the path. Dr. Charles Spielberger is here, too, to explain anxiety further.

JOURNEY GUIDE

Charles Spielberger

Examined the differences between state and trait anxiety.

Spielberger presented a deeper look into anxiety in its various forms and differentiated between state and trait anxiety. State anxiety is specifically situational. Trait anxiety tends to be more stable over time.

Fear differs from anxiety. Anxiety is a general state of apprehension, while fear has a specific object.

Two female warriors, Dr. Cousino Klein and Dr. Shelley Taylor,[8] have information to share about how stress affects women differently than men.

JOURNEY GUIDES

Cousino Klein & Shelley Taylor

These researchers studied the effects of stress on women and found dramatic differences in the responses between men and women.

Following five decades of research that studied the effects of stress on men, Klein and Taylor, along with researchers, Lewis, Gruenewald, Gurung, and Updegraff, studied women under stress. What they discovered is that in addition to the fight or flight hormonal response, oxytocin is also released. In women, oxytocin buffers the fight or flight response, and instead, makes women want to gather together with other women and tend children. That leads to greater calming and is further enhanced by estrogen.

Men, however, produce high levels of testosterone while under stress, reducing the effects of the oxytocin. (They didn't mention if it's the same factor that keeps men from asking for directions.)

Another princely guide has joined the group. It's Dr. Stephan Rechtshaffen.[9]

JOURNEY GUIDE

Stephan Rechtshaffen

*Physician and founder of the Omega Institute for Holistic
Studies and author of* Timeshifting: Creating More Time
to Enjoy Your Life.

Addressing this notion that we're not all being chased by dragons every moment, Rechtshaffen proposes that approximately ninety-five percent of the stress that we experience in our lives is related to a perception of "time poverty." This is the belief that there's not enough time to accomplish all that's required or desired by us. Maybe we shouldn't view this as life-threatening.

Rechtshaffen states, "Fear of what may come in the future provokes anxiety, the offspring of stress, which comes from resistance to being with what is in the present." He states, "In the present moment there is no stress."

How brilliant is that? When the dragon is actually chasing us, we don't stand there in our ascots, pipe to mouth saying, "My goodness, this is a stressful situation!" No. We react and prepare to either fight or flee. When the stressful event is over, we calm down, but when the reaction to stress is continual and a result of our own doing (unconsciously until now) we can work ourselves into quite an unnecessary frenzy and stay at that heightened level as our new default setting.

The biological experiment that Dr. R. describes below offers an astounding illustration of the ways in which people accept an increase in stress, by degrees, until it reaches a level that is unbearable, and causes a breakdown in the system.

If you take a frog and drop it into a pan of scalding water, he'll jump out immediately. If, however, you place him in a pan of cold water and heat it slowly, all the way to the boiling point, the frog never jumps. Because the heat is turned up gradually, the frog adjusts, little by little and doesn't react even when the water turns deadly.

Work that must be completed, according to a timetable, can turn into boiling water. Why do you think they call them deadlines? You might be the one who cranks up the heat yourself, without even realizing it.

Take a moment to consider how you have played a part in building stress mountains out of molehills. The way you talk to yourself and the meaning you assign to events need to change. This is where your choices are crucial.

When your blood starts pumping and your heart races because someone at work suggests that you should've already completed a project, you can let your body know that it doesn't have to fire up into the dragon-chasing drill, and simply disarm the alarm. Breathe. Release physical tension. Talk to yourself in a positive manner. Keep your focus and don't get sucked into other people's negative energy vortex.

When was the last time that you let another person's opinion affect you emotionally? Write down the circumstances, the person's name, his or her relationship to you, and your response. Now, rewrite the way you might have handled it that would result in a positive outcome.

PHYSICAL REACTION: Your body's response through neural, glandular or hormonal changes.
You can reprogram these alarms so that you're not kept in a constant state of high alert. Many learned behaviors trigger these reactions and you can retrain yourself to respond differently.

I'm sure you've witnessed the difference in a toddler's response to falling down, based on the mother's reaction. The toddler whose mother shrieks, clutches her chest, and rushes to pick up her child, while saying, "I'll carry you so you don't fall down again," learns to view this normal developmental process as something to be feared and avoided.

The toddler whose mother sits calmly but attentively and says, "Oops, you fell. Stand up again," and applauds when the child stands upright, will likely have a different experience. Long after the incident has been forgotten, the internal alarm sounds to whichever code has been programmed. The more a particular response is repeated, the more it is reinforced.

Adrenaline gets a lot of press and deserves its own mention here.

Adrenaline: A hormone produced by the adrenal glands, which sit on top of the kidneys.

The medical term for adrenaline is epinephrine.

Our ancestors were often faced with physical dangers, and the fight-or-flight response provided them with a mechanism for survival. For most Americans, this response was experienced during the frightening and tragic events in the United States on September 11, 2001. Just prior to that incident, many perceived dangers had been created internally. By comparison to today's stress, the stress of fifty or sixty years ago seems manageable. But even then, Seyle was quoted as saying, "The daily worries of modern life, keep our minds in a state of fear, worry, and anxiety and our bodies in a state of activation and physiologic stress."

Picture this: A fire-breathing dragon pursuing you. Let me tell you what your smart body does, involuntarily, when it perceives a life-threatening stressor: it sweats, your heart races, and blood pressure rises. You breathe faster. Blood pumps into your muscles and increases the oxygen to your lungs and heart. Your blood thickens so that if you're injured, you won't bleed out as quickly. Your body dumps sugar into your bloodstream to be used as energy. Your blood flows to your major organs to offer them extra help and doesn't worry about making it to your hands and feet, or your stomach that's trying to digest the peanut butter-and-jelly sandwich churning in it.

Waste gets secreted from the body to make it lighter. The secretion of adrenaline, allows you to take a fighter's stance, or turn and run like the wind. By the way, flow to the parts of the brain that control speech is deemed insignificant in the priority line-up of who gets the blood. That's why you often can't scream when you're extremely scared or are experiencing an adrenaline rush during a nightmare. (More good party-chat.)

Other stress hormones are released, as well as endorphins, which are your body's natural painkillers. Your pupils dilate and your ability to hear is heightened, to offer you the best possible chance for survival. Your body's amazing and busy, isn't it?

Problems arise when you go through all of this because you dropped your contact lens in the sink, rather than only when being chased by a dragon. Adrenaline is part of a compound group of catecholamines, which show up in the blood of people who experiences chronic stress.

Strain: The breakdown, over time, which occurs when you resist change or readjustment to a situation. You've heard people say, "I'm under a little strain right now." The amount of strain doesn't matter as much as how intensely you experience the demand to change. Just like when you have a strained ligament, if you don't rest it, tend to it and alter the pressure you put on it, it'll get worse. Same thing with emotional stress fractures. Whether you notice it in your body first, in your feelings, or through feedback from others, you can be sure it's an alarm that's signaling you to pay attention to the way you're thinking about or doing things.

Focus on Your Body's Stress Signals

Time to get personal. Do a quick check of your Avenues of Stress right now. Itemize what you're claiming at this stop. As we go on, you may add to your claims (or erase them!) Step under the stress detector. Scan yourself to determine what kind of stress you've got.

- Are you suffering from external stress? (Is it the "good" or "bad" variety?)
- How about environmental stress? Are you exposed to any toxins or clutter?
- List your nutritional stress. What percentage of your diet includes healthy choices? Do you abuse drugs, alcohol, or tobacco? Do you eat too many fatty foods or too much salt? Are you drinking enough water? (Divide your weight in half and that's how many ounces of water/healthy fluids you're supposed to consume daily.)
- What kind of physical stress do you have? How have you been sleeping lately? Is your body's elimination of waste in balance? Are you carrying any tension in your body right now? Where?
- How are you doing internally? Are your emotions or attitudes whacked out? (By the way, you can't do this wrong so don't add to your emotional stress with this worry.) This is where attitudes play a role in individual responses to perceived stress. Is your emotional stress temporary or on-going?

Now that you've determined what kind of stress you have, ask yourself how your body lets you know that you're under stress. Do you get headaches or stomachaches? Are your shoulders lodged in your ears? Does your voice sound pinched? Do you squint? Are your hands or teeth clenched? Is your breathing labored or shallow? Do you awaken during the night in a hot or cold sweat, with your heart pounding?

Think about the feedback you receive from others. How do they know when you're stressed? (They do know without your telling them and will be more than happy to share their perceptions if you ask.)

As your Enchantress, I assure you that I'm not asking you to go anywhere I haven't already gone. What follows is an example of the above assessment. (Okay, yes, it's mine at the moment.) The visual aid of writing yours out makes it clearer than keeping it in your head, body, or emotions.

SAMPLE ASSESSMENT:

EXTERNAL: Distress due to <u>time-poverty</u>. (I'm writing as fast as I can.)

Environmental: some <u>clutter </u>in kids' rooms needs to be cleared.

Nutritional: 99% healthy choices. No drugs, alcohol or tobacco use. No salt or fatty foods. (Okay, except for the Toll House chocolate chip cookies I made.) <u>Water intake</u> is never what it ultimately should be.

Physical stress: Sleeping well, but not late enough, due to new puppy. Magnesium and more raw foods have balanced elimination. (More than you wanted to know!)

INTERNAL: <u>Emotions</u> a little whacked out because I'm having a dinner party and wanted to try the recipes in advance but didn't have time.

PHYSICAL REACTION: Current <u>tension</u> in neck, shoulders, jaw. <u>Shallow breathing. </u>I mostly   exhale; forgetting to inhale deeply.

FEEDBACK FROM OTHERS: I observe myself multi-tasking like crazy to make up for "lost time." When my husband and kids see me doing that, they tell me to relax and calm myself. (Enchantresses are people, too!)

TEMPORARY: New puppy and pressure on myself to make the perfect meal.

LONG-TERM PATTERN: Need to watch breathing, stay on top of clutter and continue to go to bed on time.

It's very important to give yourself a star and a hug for all of the things that you are doing well at the moment. An underline of the things that need improvement is all that's necessary to heighten awareness in the unbalanced categories. This could be an opportunity for your dragon to get out a wide-tipped red permanent marker to underline all of your <u>mistakes</u> and <u>nasty habits</u>. Don't let that happen.

This is a general assessment of your current level of stress, with some hints about longer-term patterns. As you receive specific keys, you'll gather more information about yourself, along with tools for improvement.

Establish an Action to Disarm the Alarms

This will begin the process designed to change your negative habits and reinforce your positive ones. When your stress alarms sound, it's your job to turn them off. What an empowering concept. Do you have any idea how often we expect other people to make them stop? Perhaps long ago, when your alarms tripped, no one was available to help you make sense of what happened. As a result, you may have just run away with your hands over your ears (or your heart) and, rather than learning to disarm the alarms, decided it was safer to be numb to them, or pretend they didn't exist.

The action involves the following steps:

- Reconnect to yourself so that you're aware that an alarm has been activated.
- Identify the avenues or causes of the stress and how your body reacts to them.
- Take note of what steps you're following to deal with them (or not) and then consciously choose action to disarm the alarms.

Disarming an alarm is like releasing a Charlie-horse in your calf muscle during the night. You have to stretch in the opposite direction to make it stop. If your stress has been created by a negative thought, you must replace it with a positive one. If your body is stressed from eating poor quality food, you need to eat well, and so on. It's all about awareness and practice, practice, practice. What if you mindfully chose to relax before becoming stressed or ate well and slept enough to avoid a crash and burn? What a wild idea, huh?

Right here on the journey---take a breath break; a deep and cleansing breath, in through your nose, followed by an exhale through your mouth. Take another one when you're ready—inhale and exhale. (Feel free to breathe in between the suggestions to do so.) Relax the muscles in your belly. Roll your head around in a circle a few times. (Does it sound like you're crunching into peanut brittle? It shouldn't.) Now roll your head the other way. Pull your shoulders up as you inhale and let them drop as you exhale. Again. I'll wait. Squeeze your eyes shut and open them wide and then relax them. See how much stress you were holding in your body that wasn't necessary? Dear, you're on an enchanted journey, for heaven's sake, not being chased by a dragon. Relax. Let the last remnants of that tension release. Don't you feel better? You just need to do this for the rest of your life.

Wait. Did I hear mocking dragon laughter from deep in the Dragon Pit of Negativity? You *can* do this for the rest of your life. Whenever you think of it throughout your day, quickly scan your physical body and notice if you're holding tension anywhere. If so, take a moment, or several, to breathe into those tense places. Cleanse and purify your body on the inhale and release tension on the exhale. Be aware of any stress, negative thoughts or feelings you may encounter. Stop, breathe into them, release, and continue.

You'll need all your strength to walk the narrow path by the Dragon Pit of Negativity. Ready?

Chapter Four: Dragons

Stay close. We're on their turf now. Dragons are powerful. For centuries, the symbol of the dragon has played an important role in various cultures. Many authors, such as Asimov, Bradbury, Burroughs, King, and Tolkien, to name a few, have been preoccupied with dragons. Some dragons symbolize judgment, power and mystery. Others represent the material hidden from conscious awareness, tribal and cultural taboos, or the unexpressed emotions of anger, rage and sexuality untamed, unleashed, or lurking beneath the surface.

Kabat-Zinn, whom you've already met, suggests that dragons represent external factors, such as job stress or feelings of failure that show up as impotence or powerlessness.

Critical Dragon

Critical Dragon is the most common, garden-variety dragon who squashes the spirit and squelches enchantment. It's your internal critic who thrives in an atmosphere of negative self-talk. You may hear inside of your head, "You're so stupid," "You'll never be able to...," or "You can't..."

Others may have downloaded Critical Dragon into your system; however, you get to decide whether or not you wish to continue to feed and empower it or tame and retrain it. Critical Dragon is also the keeper of old wounds and excess baggage. The voice of your Critical Dragon may become deafening as you attempt to make changes. Dragons hate change. They'll tell you that journaling and meditation are a waste of time. They'll try to convince you that honoring yourself with a nap when you're sleep-deprived contributes to your laziness. That's a double-whammy—now, not only are you lazy, but tired, too.

Surprisingly, the goal is not to slay Critical Dragon.

As your Enchantress, I'll continue to signal the wounded areas within that need healing. This will help you develop a loving energy, inside of yourself, an Internal Enchantress to counter the negative messages you receive from Critical Dragon. You'll catch your balance, without falling into the Pit, and will begin to validate yourself—maybe for the first time ever. You'll be able to integrate past experiences, present awareness, and future choices, in response to yourself and others. You'll not only allow enchantment, but also invite it. Yay, you!

Recognizing the Dragons Within

Some dragons are trapped inside of you, and can impair your ability to realize your own aspirations. You may get stuck in your past experiences by continually repeating negative patterns of thought processes and behavior. Now is the time to release those dragons.

It's good to see that our special Guides show up wherever they are needed. Not one to shy away from dragons, Dr. Carl Jung[10] is present.

JOURNEY GUIDE

Carl Jung

Swiss psychiatrist and founder of Analytical Psychology known as Jungian Psychology. He believed we're more than our past experiences and are influenced by our own aspirations. Balance and harmony are key points.

Narrow-mindedness is a common trait of dragons. Jung possessed the opposite trait of expansive thinking. He set out to understand the psyche through his exploration of dreams, art, mythology, world religion and philosophy. Ignore the screaming dragons. Jung emphasized the importance of balance and harmony, and believed that we rely too heavily on science and logic and would benefit from integrating spirituality and appreciation of the unconscious realm.

Jung focused on taking an optimistic viewpoint and the creative side of humans that strives for wholeness. He embraced the unconscious mind as a resource for development and growth. That's simply what I'm asking you to do. No problema.

Jungian psychology focuses on the systems that involve "ego, personal unconscious, collective unconscious, the persona, the anima and animas, the shadow and the self." Critical Dragon is a counterpart to the "shadow" side of human nature. The shadow is the part of the personality that most of us would rather pretend doesn't exist. It's the deeply rooted, primitive and instinctual archetype. Please don't think of it as a "dark" or "evil" side, though. It's also the wellspring of creativity and spontaneity. This is why we don't want to slay our dragons. If you kill the negative parts of dragon, you also kill the good parts. Taming and retraining are the goals.

Another underpinning of Gestalt therapy that our dear friend, Perls, focused on is the notion of "unfinished business." Critical Dragon often brings up past mistakes that can thwart forward movement. Perls believed that self-defeating behaviors result from ignoring them. Having unfinished business is like dragging a live wire around behind you. It sparks along the ground and can ignite into a fire-breathing dragon.

Philosopher and author, Ken Wilbur,[11] has further wisdom that supports integration of the dragon, rather than elimination.

JOURNEY GUIDE

Ken Wilbur

A deep thinker whose concept of inclusion, transformation, and transcendence is critical to evolution.

Wilbur recognizes wholes in systems that become part of greater wholes. He describes "dominant hierarchies" as a part that usurps its position and attempts to dominate the whole, like a cancer cell does to the body. Critical Dragons can become pathological and, eventually, destroy an entire organism.

Take a deep breath. I'm not trying to scare you. Here's what you need to do. Using Wilbur's theory of integration, go *beyond* what went before (Critical Dragon pushing you around) and *embrace* it. Then you can *transcend* and *include* it.

For example, if you've been a doormat and your negative self-talk from your dragon supports that position, you would go beyond the habit and embrace all the ways in which you've been a doormat. You'd develop compassion and embrace the self that thought it was a good idea, on some level, to be a doormat. Maybe at one point you thought it would make you likable or popular. You'd then transcend the old doormat behaviors and select new ones that would include the original intent. So, you might still want to be liked or popular, but would find healthier and more satisfying ways to include those basic desires, without continuing to be a doormat.

Dr. Ann Nunley[12] created a process of healing that takes place in the presence of these dragons.

JOURNEY GUIDE

Ann Nunley

*Educator, artist, and author, developed
The Symbolic Visualization Process
from earlier research done by Vernon Wolf.*

The Symbolic Visualization Process, a powerful healing tool, combines sensations and feelings in the body along with symbolic visualization to tap into old patterns of responding to things. With regard to dragons, we could step back and say, "Oh, I get it. You wanted me to react that way (being nasty to others or ignoring them) for a reason." Linking these behaviors to specific instances, recognizing the location these wounds are stored in the physical body and psyche, assigning them a shape and color, and an exit point, allows transformation of the old patterns.

Once the old reactive thought form is accepted and validated, then the need underneath is discovered. "Oh, I've treated people this way for protection." The reason it was there in the first place is acknowledged and a different response is selected.

Dr. Deepak Chopra,[13] oncologist and visionary, known for his beliefs in healing through the mind-body connection, honors us with his presence.

JOURNEY GUIDE

Deepak Chopra

*His study of quantum physics and the importance of
meditation and self-awareness are key components in
healing.*

Chopra's beliefs about illness and healing have their foundation from his native India. Wisdom is received from the ancient *rishis*, or seers, in India, through the Veda. Chopra describes the Veda as an immense expansion of the human mind or the total content of the cosmic computer. "All the input of nature is channeled into it, and out of it flows all natural phenomena." From the Veda, rishis have brought the message, "What you see you become." Chopra states that this is a literal process, and that "just the experience of perceiving the world makes you what you are, that this truth shapes the whole physiology, including the brain." This statement urges us to recognize the voice of Critical Dragon so that we do not become the embodiment of the self-criticizing messages.

Chopra's twist on the original message is that what we think about the most, we become. Can you imagine how damaging it is to constantly feed on negative fuel? Even if you've begun your life being fed negativity, you can change what you consume (whether it's poisoned food or poisoned thoughts) once you start feeding yourself.

We're more than half way through the dragon pit. Hang in there. When we exit this area, we'll stop on safe ground to fluff your aura in case any dragons have latched on and decided to follow you.

Leonard Pearlin, Ph.D. in Sociology, professor and lecturer, along with Cami Schooler, Ph.D. in Psychology,[14] have a warning about self-esteem.

JOURNEY GUIDES

Pearlin & Schooler

Research team who studied the relationship between stress and self-concept.

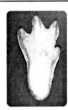

Dragon Alert!

The dragons are dancing the hula in skimpy outfits and singing in your ear to distract you. They don't want you to know about Pearlin and Schooler's research. I'll talk louder. The study was about stress and coping resources. The relationship to self-concept played a significant role. Three psychological traits turned out to be crucial in their relationship to stress. These were self-esteem, self-denigration, and mastery.

Can you hear me, now? Self-denigration proved to be the strongest variable for all four of the major life arenas assessed in the study. Stress was greater for those who were most likely to have negative thoughts about themselves in these four major areas of life: marital, parenting, financial and work.

Scan your four areas and check out your level of stress in each. Any negative messages in there about yourself? We'll start to clear them in just a minute.

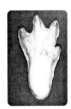

Dragon Alert!

Another one so soon! Close call. We almost got run off the road. That was Critical Dragon behind the wheel. Yes. Dragons in their glory, with the whole issue of road rage, are often in the drivers' seat. Many of you are nodding in recognition. Whether these are your dragons to claim and retrain or to steer clear of, this stuff is crucial to know.

Unfortunately, many people who consider themselves intelligent, rational, and even spiritual, may recognize the presence of Critical Dragon sitting on their laps while driving. As the roadways become increasingly congested, road rage and aggressive driving increases. Driving has become a stressful and dangerous experience. Every year there are approximately fifty-thousand roadway deaths and about three million injuries. It appears that aggressive driving has become a cultural norm handed down to the tiniest of passengers in the vehicle. This habit is observed by children and reinforced by the media with television programs, movies and music videos in which people are driving aggressively.

Experts on the topic of road rage, such as Dr. Leon James, Professor and Ph.D. in psychology, along with Dr. Diane Nahl,[15] Ph.D. in Communication and Information Sciences, offer their insight.

JOURNEY GUIDES

> # Leon James & Diane Nahl
>
> *Educators and lecturers in the field of Traffic Psychology and road rage. Developed DrDriving as the inner voice that counters the actions of road warriors (aka dragons).*

James would like you to know that he's a former road warrior. His wife, the brave and courageous, Diane Nahl, took a deep breath and confirmed her ninety-two year old mother's assessment that Leon wasn't a good driver. She communicated this to him and the outcome led to combined work in this field of traffic psychology, which offers a change in attitude and perception through interpersonal skills. The principles of this theory include qualities of "chivalry, charity, freedom, family values, citizenship and respect for law and order, spirituality, morality and rationality, empathy and sympathy, national unity and integration, and creative driving practices."

DrDriving became a friendly driving coach from within that James needed in order to "steer clear of aggressive driving." (Internal Enchantress is a wonderful driving coach as well.) DrDriving.org is a website created by James and Nahl. Their books and articles on driving psychology are posted, as well as survey results and collections of road rage news and legislation. We would do well, as a society, to adopt these principles, and teach them to our children.

Richard Carlson, Ph.D. in Psychology,[16] whose humor and perspective will assist us all along the way, also offers reasons to reduce aggressive attitudes and behaviors while driving.

JOURNEY GUIDE

> # Richard Carlson
> *Psychotherapist, motivational speaker, and author of one of many best-selling books, including*
> Don't Sweat the Small Stuff…and it's all Small Stuff

The first reason Carlson has for reducing aggression on the road addresses the physical danger to the self and others. Secondly, the focus is on the physiological effects on the driver, including increased blood pressure, muscle tension, eyestrain and emotional responses.

Abraham Maslow,[17] emerges in order to share the concept of self-actualization, which can become a goal for all of us. (Self-actualized people usually try not to practice road rage.)

JOURNEY GUIDE

Abraham Maslow

*A psychologist noted for his proposal of a hierarchy of
needs, with self-actualization at the top. He is considered
to be the father of humanistic psychology.*

Maslow viewed the needs of human beings as if arranged on a ladder. At the bottom are the basic
psychological needs of air to breathe, food to eat, water, sleep, a state of equilibrium, the body's
elimination and sex. Then there are the *safety* needs of security; personal, family, and job security, safety
of health and property. Next, are the psychological needs for *love* and *belonging*. Then there is the need
for esteem; respect for self and others and a sense of confidence and accomplishment. Finally, at the top
of the ladder are the *self-actualizing* needs that lead us to be moral, creative, spontaneous, thinking,
feeling, and accepting of people—for the self and others, capable of becoming all that we can.

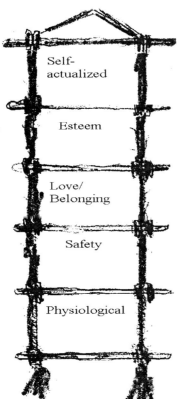

Maslow is a very important guide to walk with because self-actualization is
at the polar opposite end of the Dragon Pit. As we move up the ladder, out of the pit, we become more
versatile in our capacity to experience, as well as to express, the full range of human capabilities. When
people are hungry, a basic need, they aren't contemplating the nature of the Universe. They are looking
for food. Once the belly is fed, then they may progress up the ladder. When self-actualization is reached,
there's a balance between inner perceptions and outward expressions.

We gain an awareness that encompasses past, present and future experiences. In other words, we
move away from critical self-talk and from flipping off others whom we perceive to be in our way. We
learn to feed, clothe, and provide shelter for ourselves. We ascend to higher thoughts and actions,

observing ourselves in the context of our worlds, and making choices that improve the quality of our lives and the lives of those around us.

Whew. Let's curl up like children on nap mats for a moment.

Speaking of kids, Dr. Meg Eastman, author and child psychologist, along with co-author, Sydney Craft Rozen,[18] recognized the dragons inside children and work to tame them.

JOURNEY GUIDES

Eastman & Rozen

*They focus on the connection between negative self-talk
and signs of stress in the physical body,
present even in young children.*

The title of Eastman and Rozen's book, *Taming the Dragon in Your Child: Solutions for Breaking the Cycle of Family Anger* suggests that this internal dragon is alive and well in childhood and challenged by untamed anger. This connection between negative self-talk and signs of stress is acknowledged and reframed as opportunities for self-monitoring.

Eastman and Rozen created an exercise for children that we all can use, called The Rage Gauge. It allows children who are anxious and highly stressed, to recognize when they need to implement cooldown strategies. (This may be one reason that children aren't allowed to drive.) A primary strategy is positive self-talk, accompanied by physical relaxation. Self-defeating thoughts get replaced with positive coping statements.

They also offer "pressure breaks." These are preventative measures that provide opportunities to release pressure before it becomes unmanageable. Who doesn't need that? Eastman and Rozen suggest that the rewards given for self-management include "more time for play, humor and relaxation." In addition, these wise women advise the parents of children who are out of control to keep their communications brief, in order to avoid feeding the dragon. It's important for each of us to discover what fuels the fire in our dragons.

Another gracious Queen appears; Dr. Wendy Mogel,[19] clinical psychologist, parent educator and author.

JOURNEY GUIDE

Wendy Mogel

*She utilizes Jewish teachings to raise self-reliant children
who don't just feel good, but are taught to be good people.*

In her book, *The Blessing of a Skinned Knee,* Mogel references the *yetzer hara* and the *yetzer tov.* The *yetzer hara* is defined as the "impulse for evil" (on the curriculum vitae for dragons) and the *yetzer tov* as the "impulse for good," which, it's believed, everyone is endowed with at birth.

Mogel supports the idea that the *yetzer hara* is not to be destroyed, but controlled and channeled. She suggests that it's necessary for human survival, manifested as the "spark" or "zip" in life. Mogel states, "We live fully by balancing two forces: our burning passions and our ability to exercise self-restraint." Without the vigor of the *yetzer hara*, "there would be no marriages, no children conceived, no homes built, and no businesses." It's a good reminder that dragons who are full of themselves can run amok, but those in check, can be quite valuable to have around.

STORY: Cherokee Grandfather's Wisdom

In Native American tradition, there's a similar Cherokee teaching. It's told as a story of a grandfather instructing his grandson about life. The grandfather explains to the boy that there's a terrible fight going on inside of him, between two wolves. He describes one wolf as evil, embodying anger, envy, sorrow, regret, greed, arrogance, self-pity, resentment, inferiority, lies, false pride, superiority and ego. The other wolf is described as good, embracing the qualities of joy, peace, love, serenity, humility, kindness, benevolence, empathy, generosity, truth, compassion and faith. He explains to the boy that the same fight is going on inside of him, too, and every other person there is. After some thought, the boy asks his grandfather which wolf will win and the old, wise Cherokee man replies simply, "The one you feed."

Good job. You can put your pen and journal down for now. Stretch, get comfortable, and I'll tell you a story about a previous tour group that I accompanied on The Enchanted Journey.

STORY: The University Students

I led a tour, just like yours, of university students, who were about to become educators in kindergarten through fifth grade. No stress there.

When asked to write down a stressful situation that was currently being experienced by each of the students, a volunteer offered that she was nervous about student teaching. The written exercise that follows is the internal criticism from her Critical Dragon, the imagined positive response from me, The Enchantress and then her reply as her own Internalized Enchantress.

Stressful situation: "I'm nervous about student teaching."

CRITICAL DRAGON: (the internal criticism)

"You should be nervous! You're not going to be able to control them. You'll probably start crying, like always, and won't know what to do. What are you going to do when you find out that you're a lousy teacher?"

1. **THE ENCHANTRESS**: (the validation)

"You're just scared because you want to do a good job and you've never done this before. You'll get better at it as you have more experience."

   2. **INTERNALIZED ENCHANTRESS**: (validate yourself and plan an action)

"Of course I'm scared. I can take a deep breath and slow things down. I might be able to have an assistant in the room if I decide that I need one. I can plan strategies, in advance, for how I'll deal with behavioral issues. I'll be a good teacher. I am a good teacher already."

Thanks to this brave volunteer, another tourist sorted out her experience with her dragons. Her stressful situation follows:

Stressful situation: "I procrastinate when I'm given an assignment for school. Then I push myself beyond comfortable or healthy limits, in order to complete it on time."

1. CRITICAL DRAGON: (the internal criticism)

"You must be really smart if you can pull it off in the eleventh hour. It's an even bigger accomplishment to do it that way."

(Support of a negative habit is another way Critical Dragon tricks and trips you.)

   2. **THE ENCHANTRESS**: (the validation)

"Yes, you're smart. And you don't have to go to such great lengths to prove it. Do you know where that pattern comes from?"

   3. **INTERNALIZED ENCHANTRESS**: (validate yourself and plan an action)

"I had a childhood belief that I needed to do more than my sister to be noticed and accepted by my parents. They know I'm smart and, more importantly, I know it. It's too stressful to do my assignments at the last minute, so I'm going to make a timeline in which to complete them."

DRAGON CLEARING

So, as you consider your dragons and the dragons of those you interact with, you may notice that Critical Dragon seems very familiar. Why don't we climb out of the pit, find some solid ground, and spend a few moments reflecting on your dragons? Then, during your free time, you may gently step across the drawbridge to open discussions with others about theirs.

Activities: (You will need your pen and journal.)

Targeting Stressful Areas in your Mind: (self-talk with the dragons)

Look all around to see if any dragons have glommed on to you, before beginning.

1. Write down what you know about your dragons.

   Example: <u>YOU</u>: "My Critical Dragon keeps me from reaching out to make new friends and tells me I don't sing well, even though I love to sing."

2. **Consider how you feel about this, if the only feelings are mad, sad, glad, and scared.** (All the other words are just fancy variations of these feelings. By the way, anxiety usually falls in the "scared" category and depression in the "sad" category.)

   Example: <u>YOU</u>: "I feel sad about this."

3. **Internalize The Enchantress, to offer validation and acknowledgement of your feelings. This is your journey---make it the ideal one. Allow further exploration.**

   Example:

THE ENCHANTRESS: "You feel sad about this. Is it because you feel lonely and fear criticism?

(Hint: You might call Maslow in for help with your position on the ladder.) What do you need?"

YOU: "Yes, I do feel alone and not everybody has a great singing voice. Mine isn't terrible, though. Looking at the ladder, I need both a sense of belonging and, on the esteem rung, some self-confidence."

THE ENCHANTRESS: "Good! Here's a magic wand. What would you need to do to try and solve this problem?"

YOU: "I need to balance my fear of rejection with my desire to be connected to others. I have to try to reach out, even if every attempt doesn't result in a lasting friendship. I'd also like to sing, just for fun, while listening to music with others, without worrying that they're judging me. I want to understand the reasons I judge myself so harshly, pat myself gently on the heart, and let them go."

THE ENCHANTRESS: "Yay, for you!"

4. List the people in your life who side with the dragons.

Who supports your negative and critical view of yourself? This is tough to look at because these people may also be those you love or who love you. People on different rungs of the ladder than you may operate out of their wounds.

5. List those who support the expression of your inner self.

Who backs you when you stand up for yourself and takes pride in your achievements, skills and talents in a balanced and appropriate way?

6. What are the messages you received in childhood that your Critical Dragon still repeats to you today?

7. What do you usually do with the awareness that you are hearing from your Critical Dragon?

Do you cave in and agree with it, becoming anxious or depressed? Do you rear up and breathe fire on others? Do you develop physical symptoms of distress or disease?

8. What is the loudest negative message your Critical Dragon repeats that you would like to change?

9. What current situation is stressful for you?

10. What does your dragon have to say about it?

11. What do you think The Enchantress would say about it?

12. What action would you like to take to change things?

You can begin to see how plugging your stress into various formulas for dissolution is useful. Now that we've explored the stress in your mind, and a couple of other people's lives, let's pay attention to the stress in your emotions and physical body.

Targeting Stressful Areas in your Emotions and Physical Body:

(What you do with the messages you receive from your dragons.)

1. When you experience stress, what feelings are most likely to come up for you?

2. **Where in your physical body do you carry your stress?**
   Are you a person who experiences stomach tension when stressed? Do you raise your shoulders into your ears? Do you get headaches?

3. **Looking back, how did you experience your stress in childhood?**

4. **Does the way you experience your stress now change with the cause of your stress?**
   In other words, is what you do with your stress different, depending upon whether it's in response to your children, your job, friends, or situations?

5. **Ask five people who are close to you to describe what they observe about you when you're stressed.**
   (My children taught me that when I'm stressed my voice raises several octaves to a pitch that only small animals can hear.)

Action Plan

Use this plan when you realize that your dragons are in charge. Check in with yourself several times throughout each day. When your Critical Dragon is ruling, you need the command to **H.E.A.L.-Halt, Evaluate, Acknowledge, and Level**. Once you become aware (with practice) that you're off balance, you can take the following steps: Immediately **Halt**, or stop, the behavior. Next, take a moment to **Evaluate** what you are experiencing in your physical body, thoughts, and emotions. **Acknowledge** the source from which this pattern was created (which can either be people or events) and then **Level.** Center yourself. Think of a seesaw being brought to balance. Ruminating about the past can tip the seesaw too far to the left and anxiety about the future can tip it too far to the right. The present is balanced in the middle. Ah.

It would certainly be reasonable to enlist the help of a professional therapist to assist you on this journey of self-discovery. There is no shame in asking others for help, no matter what your Critical Dragon has to say about it.

GATEWAY TO THE ENCHANTED KEYS

You are at the entrance to The Enchanted Keys. Consider now whether or not you'd like to change your life, forever.

If so, carry on…

A nod to Drs. Paul A. Alberto and Anne C. Troutman,[20]

JOURNEY GUIDES

Alberto & Troutman

Researchers in the field of behavior analysis in the classroom as well as the usefulness of reinforcement sampling.

Alberto and Troutman, through their research, suggest that offering multiple techniques for learning increases the likelihood that one, or more, will resonate with you. In turn, this increases the chances that you'll continue to practice the techniques that you find most desirable. This is reinforcement sampling.

The Enchanted Keys will give you an arsenal of ways to cope with stress and anxiety, and increase the enchantment in your life. Many of these techniques can be practiced in combination with one another.

Dr. Howard Gardner, [21] is a prince who broke the mold in thinking that intelligence results from a single factor and can be measured by IQ tests.

JOURNEY GUIDE

Howard Gardner

He demonstrated that people have multiple intelligences and learn best through processing information in a variety of ways.

Some of the ways in which Gardner discovered that people learn best are:
1) verbal/linguistic, 2) logical/mathematical, 3) visual/spatial, 4) bodily/kinesthetic,
5) musical/rhythmical, 6) intrapersonal, 7) interpersonal, and 8) naturalist.

Have fun and explore which of these techniques you prefer, as well as which style is most effective in helping you process the information.

Now you know what's possible. Take the next step.

The Enchanted Keys

Chapter Five: Mindfulness

Key #1

Congratulations. You've crossed the threshold to The Enchanted Keys. As you approach the path into mindfulness, you realize that you can't get there until you're there. Awareness is in the present moment. Don't ponder this too long. Just be where you are.

Mindfulness: A Brief History

The practice of mindfulness is traditionally associated with Buddhist monks and Zen Masters. It's recently been gaining popularity in Western culture. Mindfulness was originally connected to the practice of meditation, but now encompasses a much broader scope. It involves awareness that's focused on the present and includes all of the feelings, thoughts, and sensations associated with that experience. It's born out of Buddhist practice, but is also separate from it, as it doesn't subscribe to any religious observance and is more a way of paying attention that fosters self-understanding and healing. Additionally, it can lead one to a deeper realm of internal peace.

There's no God present in Buddhism, just a sage and teacher embodied in an historical figure called Buddha. It's been said that Buddha was approached and asked if he were a god. "No," he replied. "I am awake." The essence of mindfulness is aimed at awakening awareness to what is present. If what you create around you is beautiful, joyful, soulful, serene, then that is reflected in all that you do.

We've already met Kabat-Zinn, but he sits with us graciously to share his wisdom about mindfulness meditation.

JOURNEY GUIDE

> # Jon Kabat-Zinn
>
> *He describes mindfulness as the conscious, moment-to-moment focus on what one is intentionally doing, thinking and feeling.*

Kabat-Zinn found that mindfulness can be applied to a wide range of areas that cause people significant stress, including medical symptoms, physical and emotional pain, anxiety, panic, time pressures, relationships, work, food and events in the outside world.

In fact, Kabat-Zinn conducted a study that measured the effects of mindfulness training on the reduction of anxiety and panic in participants that had been diagnosed with these conditions. The subjects had to practice "non-doing" and "being" for an eight-week training period, with a three-month follow-up. Not only at the end of the training period was there a marked reduction in both anxiety and depression, but by the end of the follow-up period, nearly all of the participants were free from panic attacks.

The invitation to experience enchantment through mindfulness each and every day is expressed in the following story.

STORY: Gandhi on Vacation

A journalist had suggested to Mahatma Gandhi that, after working fifteen-hour days, every day, for nearly fifty years, perhaps it was time that he took a vacation. Gandhi replied, "I am always on vacation."

The definition of the word, vacation, means, "empty, vacant." When there is mindfulness, all of life is available at all times and there is no time. Time is empty and there is a detachment from it. Kabat-Zinn suggests that if this concept were practiced all year long, people might have even better vacations.

Thich Nhat Hanh,[22] Vietnamese monk, poet, peace activist and teacher has much to share with us about mindfulness.

JOURNEY GUIDE

Thich Nhat Hanh

He teaches that the path through suffering may lead one to a deeper appreciation of what is present.

STORY: Mindfulness

While in the process of becoming an Enchantress, I attended an Omega Institute conference. The founder, Dr. Stephan Rechschaften (the frog and boiling water), shared his awakening of the true practice of mindfulness in the presence of Thich Nhat Hanh. It had a profound effect on me when he told a story about the two of them, each who had been lecturing at the Omega Institute. They had a short time for a meal break and as Stephan raced across the grass to the dining hall, he encountered Thich and hurriedly asked him what he was doing. He stated that Thich replied, "Me? I am walking." Stephan further explained that had he been asked, he would've responded by saying he was going to the dining hall, by-passing his current experience completely.

Most of us stay so focused on our destination that we forget the path along the way. It's the experience of this path that enriches our lives, and our Critical Dragons who fool us into believing that getting "there" is all that matters.

Mindfulness walking, for instance, involves being present while walking. It's the observance of breath and the ground beneath your feet. There might be pebbles on the path or it might be smooth. There may be a flower by the side of the road, a butterfly, or a penny. You're all familiar with those roses you're supposed to remember to stop and smell.

Conversations offer another arena in which to practice mindfulness. Have you ever experienced forgetting the person's name that just introduced him or herself to you because you were so busy getting your name right? Chances are that you didn't forget as much as that you weren't really listening. Maybe you were time traveling into the future, when it would be your turn to introduce yourself, and so you weren't even there when you were told the name. This also happens in conversations. Whether the discussion is one about politics or romance it would be beneficial to stay present with your own experience, as well as the position and experience of others.

A Problem

Have you ever felt pulled between conflicting thoughts? When you're at work, do you think about being at home (with or without children) and when at home, are you thinking about work? People do this with vacations all of the time; think about them constantly while at work, and then once on vacation, obsess about what's going on at the office. (Is this you?)

Sometimes conflicting emotions arise. Even during activities that are desired, there can be a split between being present and having a focus somewhere else.

For instance, one tourist shared with me that she feels angry once she's engaged in reading to her children. She wants to read to them but, after beginning, feels trapped and anxious. In exploring the anxiety, it was discovered that she leaves the present activity of reading and spending time with them and drifts to thoughts about what's left on her to-do list for the rest of the day.

Present time is abandoned and future time is engaged. She ruminates about making dinner, serving it, eating it, cleaning up, getting the kids bathed, to bed, sewing a hem, watching the news, and dropping off into an exhausted, coma-like sleep. Can you imagine the stress meter if one of her children asks to hear *The Hungry Caterpillar* one more time?

Then there's the guilt and fearful thoughts that this neglected child will be sitting in front of a therapist in twenty years, trying to understand what he did wrong by asking to hear the story a second time.

A Solution

A short period of time spent planning the future can alleviate the stress in the present. Set boundaries for yourself and others. Take a moment to decide that perhaps thirty minutes, either then or at a specified time, will be devoted to reading to the children. Then there's a boundary around it that can allow you to be fully present in the experience. When you're only wearing one hat at a time, it's easier to be focused.

Julie Morgenstern[23] is an author and mother who understands how to manage time and clutter, in order to achieve the Zen of internal and external space.

JOURNEY GUIDE

Julie Morgenstern
Best-selling author and speaker who shares her wisdom about time and organization management. She helps others create places in the daily schedule for important activities with self and others.

Morgenstern's books, *Time Management From the Inside Out, Organizing from the Inside Out: The Foolproof System for Organizing Your Home, Your Office and Your Life, Never Check E-mail in the Morning,* and others, help people get organized and productive. Once some time is spent in the planning phase there is freedom within the boundaries to enjoy each event. It takes some practice to keep your mind in the present, but the rewards are worth it.

I think You-Know-Who is the one telling you that if you keep one foot out of whatever you're engaged in that somehow you won't lose yourself to everyone else's imposed desires. All that does is prevent you from ever being fully engaged in anything. That's not very enchanting, is it?

Activities:

Practicing Mindfulness

1. **Sit down to your next meal mindfully.** (Hopefully it will be fresh and organic.) If you are having a salad, for instance, stop to think about how a particular tomato got to your table. If you didn't grow it and pick it yourself, who did? After the farmers grew and harvested it, how did it get to the store? Think of the time that went into arranging it so that it would look pleasing to you, how that particular tomato caught your eye and was selected to go home with you. There were a lot of forces synchronized just so you could have lunch!

2. **Eat the tomato, or whatever it is, mindfully.** Turn off the television, the computer, the telephone, the mail, the email, and the rest of the world. Look at the deep, beautiful color of the tomato. Smell it. (Here's another plug for organic gardening. It's my wish for you that you'll smell the fresh, sweet scent of the fleshy, ripe, warm tomato, rather than the pesticides on it, if it's not organic.) Listen to your tomato, not so much for instructions about how to live your life, as the sound of the juicy explosion of seeds when you slice or bite into it. Taste it. Notice its taste separately and in combination with the fresh basil and provolone cheese, drizzled with olive oil, you may have chosen to have with it. Then, experience the texture of the tomato. Notice how it's different whole than when sliced.

3. **Go for a walk.** Walk mindfully and observe how that's different from the way in which you usually walk. (Afterward, you can journal about your discoveries.)

4. **Have a mindful conversation.** Really listen. Be present. Respond from that same place within yourself. Notice how that differs from the ways in which you usually communicate.

5. **Select one area in your life in which you would like to practice mindfulness for one week.** Don't overwhelm yourself. If you choose to try this with eating, select one meal a day, for starters. You can always work up to including more (and hopefully you will!) but keep it simple and start making changes slowly. If it's in the area of allotting time to others or the self, begin with twenty to thirty minutes a day or an hour, three times a week. That'll be enough for you to discover how you'd like to tweak the boundaries.

Action Plan:

Observe the patterns you've developed that are not mindful. Think about the changes you'd like to make that can incorporate mindfulness. Remember that these choices should serve you and others in healthful ways, for the well being of body, mind, spirit and emotions. Make a list and prioritize it. Use a journal to track your awarenesses.

Congratulations! You've just received your first key.

Chapter Six: Altered Perceptions

Here, things are not always as they seem. "Bad" things may bring you insight and turn out to be "good" things. "Good" things may seem good enough but can be made even better.

Phillip L. Rice[24] author and wizard of stress management, is here with us.

JOURNEY GUIDE

Philip Rice

He presents extensive research in the field of stress management.

Rice defines perception as "the interpretation and organization of all information provided to the brain by the senses. *Interpretation* suggests that some meaning is connected to the information and a value judgment made about it."

We all perceive the world through our senses. Based on who we are, we decide whether what we've perceived is a good thing or a bad thing, even if the person next to us has a completely different take on our reality. The task at this stop is to learn how to take lemons and make lemonade.

Rest again, and I'll share another story of how altering the perception of a stressful event can be transformed into a gift. Its two main heroes are Dr. Wayne Dyer,[25] Doctorate in Education and, initially, a school counselor, and Dr. Carlson, whom you already know.

JOURNEY GUIDE

Wayne Dyer

Self-help advocate, author and lecturer in the field of psychology and spirituality.

STORY: Don't Sweat the Small Stuff

There had been a mix-up in the publishing world. Dr. Wayne Dyer had written an endorsement for an earlier book written by Dr. Richard Carlson. It was accidentally printed on the cover of his subsequent book. Carlson, himself, had specifically stated that it couldn't be used for that book without Dyer's permission. In an attempt to rectify the situation and offer apologies to Dyer, Carlson wrote a letter of explanation. Dyer's response follows: "Richard. There are two rules for living in harmony. #1) Don't sweat the small stuff and #2) It's all small stuff. Let the quote stand. Love, Wayne."

Carlson received this philosophy with gratitude that prompted him to write a best-selling book entitled: *Don't Sweat the Small Stuff...and it's all small stuff: Simple Ways to Keep the Little Things from Taking Over Your Life.*

Many nay-sayers who hold the philosophy that "life's a bitch and then you die," are afraid to imagine that their perceptions could be different because they don't want to be disappointed. Shifting perceptions is the start to changing that philosophy and moving you from there to enlightenment.

Enlightenment is generally thought of as a blissful state of consciousness, which, if attained, also brings with it a release from all earthly challenges.

Nah.

Dyer takes the viewpoint that enlightenment is not something to be attained, but something to be realized. He shares the Zen proverb with us that embodies this message:

Before enlightenment
chopping wood
carrying water
After enlightenment
chopping wood
carrying water

It seems as if after enlightenment has been achieved, everything in the world would be different. Actually, nothing is different, except the perception of the world, and that's huge. Dyer compares this process of enlightenment to a person who walks through the world with his eyes closed. Suddenly, upon opening them, the world appears to be new, when, in fact it hasn't changed. The person is simply viewing the world with open eyes and a new perspective. Dyer states that this changed perspective, also referred to as enlightenment, "is not something that you will get from a guru or a book or a course of study. Enlightenment is an attitude toward everything that you do."

Passing by, is Evelyn Underhill,[26] a Christian mystic. Her beliefs echo Dyer's.

JOURNEY GUIDE

Evelyn Underhill

She believes that living the spiritual life is not about living in a monastery or nunnery, but is "the attitude you hold in your mind when you're down on your knees cleaning the steps."

The Zen of Laundry

There is laundry on the journey.

Jokingly at first, I came up with the Zen of Laundry practice. Little did I know that after I learned about Underhill's work, I'd receive validation in my own mudroom.

Laundry is one of those cyclical tasks that offers minimal and fleeting satisfaction. As soon as the last article of clothing is folded or hung and put away, the pile begins to grow again. In laundry and in life, attitude is everything.

Clean up your dirty attitude.

So I tracked my outlook while doing laundry, as well as other repetitive tasks, such as grocery shopping, meal preparation, yard work, and brushing and flossing, to name a few. I noticed that some of these chores were enjoyable already, but others caused me to mutter audibly.

"Poor Cinderella," I called myself, until I realized that she never bemoaned her lot. In some portrayals she even whistled while performing her many chores! Who knew that Cinderella is an enlightened being; neither a pathetic doormat nor a suffering martyr?

As an E.I.T. (Enchantress in Training), I assessed that a change in my attitude was in order. I couldn't ask you to do this if I hadn't already done it myself. Instead of complaining about my laundry, which, by the way, took place in a lovely, sunlit room with conditioned air and state-of-the-art appliances, I shifted my attention to the people who don't have clothes to wash or those who are ill and unable to perform the most mundane tasks; people who would be thrilled to be able to do so, if given the chance.

Taking altered perceptions a step further, I kept a gratitude journal, documenting at the end of each day all that I was grateful for. Some of the previously annoying circumstances of the day were reframed as valuable lessons in self-awareness. Playing with the idea of inviting enchantment to those boring tasks became fun. Adding sensory experiences made them even better. When you receive Key #4, for Sensory Experiences, you'll understand exactly what I mean.

Guests make fun of me on these tours, sometimes, but I can take it. Laugh or groan, if you must, but I suggest that you envision yourself dancing with your basket of clean clothes. Deeply inhale the fresh fruits of your labor and caress the fibers of the garments your loved ones have worn.

I don't even think Donna Reed (wholesome, 1950s television mom) enjoyed doing laundry that much, but this will let you measure where on the scale you stand.

Change your environment.

While shifting toward the Zen of Laundry, begin with the sense of sight. What does your laundry space look like? Whether you're in your own home, you frequent the corner Laundromat or are in an apartment basement, you can enhance the experience. Is the environment cluttered, dark and uninviting? Change it. Do *something* to make it fun in there.

Your laundry room at home could be a place to use outrageous paint to define the space, or construct shelving to store cleaning products and hangers that hold the clothes as they come out of the dryer. You can stand on one of those spongy mats that help with fatigue by providing cushioning under your feet.

If you trek your laundry somewhere else, consider taking a small, brightly-colored folding chair, rolling backpack for laundry, refreshments, and a good book or portable music, to make the chore more tolerable. Keep a container for quarters by your entryway, so you don't have to scrounge around for them when it's laundry time.

That addresses the visual space. Now, for the sense of smell, decide which fragrances your clothes should exude. If you like lavender, you can add a few drops of essential oil to a spray bottle of water and mist the clothes before folding or hanging them. (Careful not to get the concentrated oil directly on the clothes, as it may stain them). Often, a misting of water helps pull out some of the wrinkles. You can light incense or a scented candle in the laundry area. Always consider safety first, please, but no dryer sheets, as they're neither good for the environment nor you.

Introduce sound so that the muttering to yourself about how annoying this task is, can be muffled. Play your favorite soothing music or, like the supermarkets do when they wish to move you through the store, play loud and lively music. Ethnic music may stir your spirit and make the task more fun.

I encounter people who feel angry and resentful, or are overwhelmed with doing their family's laundry. Some have turned the task over to others, only to discover that their favorite sweaters now fit Mini-Me. Then there are those, on the opposite end of the continuum, who starch and iron their husband's underwear. It's astounding to see how life's perceptions can appear in the armpit stains of a loved one's T-shirt.

It turns out that science has known for a long time that the attitudes we have about our circumstances define our experience of them at the most basic level. Molecules become cell receptors for the neurochemicals in our brains and our structure and chemistry become altered. Who knew?

STORY: Stress is Hard Work

I gave an Enchanted Tour at a local hospital a few years ago. A vibrant, elderly gentleman approached me, afterward. He thanked me for telling him that Hans Selye coined the term, "stress." Chuckling, he added, "In the old days, we didn't call it stress, we called it work."

This man regaled me with a tale of his youth that included sixteen-hour days spent working on his parents' farm. When he was old enough to attend school, he did so, yet still was responsible for his chores. He said, "I simply did them. I didn't tell the pigs while I was slopping them, that I was stressed out." He shared that he felt good about himself at the end of the day, when he had eaten some and thrown his tired body down onto his bed.

Shaking his head, he spoke of the "young folks" today. His daughter-in-law constantly complains about how stressed she is. She's an administrative assistant and, as he reports, becomes stressed because the phone rings constantly and she's required to talk to people for most of the day. "My *word*," he said sarcastically, in his Southern drawl. "How *does* she do it? She sits in one place all day, dressed nicely, in an air-conditioned or heated environment, never getting mud on her, and she's upset because she has to do what her job entails." He said that it would be like a doctor complaining about all of the sick people coming to see him.

In all fairness, I didn't get to talk to his daughter-in-law, but his take on the situation was crystal clear. If people would just shift their perceptions about what they're doing, for example, his suggestion to call it "work rather than stress," they would be much healthier in mind, body and attitude. We talked at length and I learned one of the best lessons in altering perceptions that I could ever imagine.

On one of my enchanted side trips, I had the pleasure of meeting Dr. Steven Vasquez,[27] a counseling psychologist and certified medical psychotherapist.

JOURNEY GUIDE

Steven Vasquez

In 1984, he developed Confluent Somatic Therapy, a synthesis of bioenergy and psychotherapy.

STORY: It Just Clicked

I attended several of Dr. Vaszquez' workshops in California, when he was compiling research on Confluent Somatic Therapy. It's a fascinating field of study that focuses on healing the attitudes that can get lodged in the physical body at the time of injury or illness.

Another attendee at the workshop volunteered to go through the process of releasing and clearing a physical injury she had experienced a few years earlier. Beginning with her current physical symptoms, she described a clicking in her kneecap when she walked. Dr. Vasquez asked her to walk so that we could all hear it click. It did. Then through a process of guided imagery, he gently took her back to the point of injury. She was on the ski slopes, having moved to a more advanced slope, after much practice and determination. Just as she felt the exhilaration of moving swiftly and deftly down the slope, she saw what she described as an inexperienced skier who was arrogant and clowning around, right in her path. Unable to veer away, she tumbled over him, hearing the crunch in her knee. After her surgery and several months of rehabilitation, she was pain-free; however, she was left with a permanent scar and the clicking sound when she walked.

It was amazing to observe Dr. Vasquez as he explored this woman's feelings of rage toward the skier. She'd earned this vacation through hard work and dedication and had set her goals for getting off the bunny slopes. The fact that this "jerk" could ruin it all because he got in her way really upset her. It was revealed that she was more upset about his attitude prior to her injury than the fact that it actually occurred. She realized that if she had caused the injury herself or if the attitude of the other skier had been serious but he had just lost control, she would've felt differently.

Simply put, Dr. Vasquez led her back, through a guided visualization, to her attitude at the time of the incident. The event itself did not change, but she was able to see how she had tucked that rage into her knee and could choose to release it. Dr. Vasquez helped facilitate a change in her perception of the event. The click in her knee ceased. I ran into her at another workshop a few months later and inquired about it. At that time she reported that it had not returned. What a powerful testimony to our ability to shift our perceptions in life.

Shakti Gawain[28] inspires us.

JOURNEY GUIDE

> # Shakti Gawain
>
> *She is a pioneer in the field of personal growth and consciousness, best known for her book,* Creative Visualization.

Gawain states: "Old values and patterns can no longer be followed. We must heal ourselves and find our own path. We must make use of our will, become valiant 'knights' on a crusade for positive thinking, positive acting. However, on this crusade we cannot become victorious unless we also recognise our shadow side; our fears, our denials, our negative thought-patterns. This side of ourselves must also be brought into the light in order to manifest wholeness."

This is a woman who sounds like she has done battle with the Dragons. I have used many of her visualizations to heal my own wounds and those of others. Visualizing various outcomes opens possibilities and allows perceptions to change.

Being able to alter perceptions helps to transform 20/20 hindsight into "present sight." You may need to examine situations from the past that you've gained clarity about, to understand what shifted and how it shifted. Then you can begin to alter perceptions in the present. The hindsight allows you to consider who you were at a given time; based on the information you had about yourself and the world around you. From this moment on, you're invited to choose differently than you ever have.

For example, if you experience stress with regard to punctuality, you may notice that you repeat several patterns that perpetuate this behavior. As you leave late, once again, you may feel angry with your boss for making you come in early. You might be angry with yourself for sabotaging your career. Maybe you're angry with your neighbor who works at home and is leisurely walking the dog while you're zooming out of the driveway. You're unconsciously creating your own stress in your life.

Altering perceptions, in this case, doesn't mean that you learn to let go of the time restraints and become joyous about being labeled "the person who's always late," (although you could choose this option.) What it does do, is allow you to consciously observe yourself in this situation and to change it. The choices that you make, based on your assessment, can reduce your stress, your negative self-concept, the perceptions of you by others, as well as your experience of the quality of your life. This seems like it's worth a try to me!

You probably already realize that your Critical Dragon is in the driver's seat. Send him or her on an errand and sit down to tea with your Internal Enchantress. Using the previous example, take a look at the underlying reason you're always late. Chances are good that you've lost or misplaced your personal power in this situation. Ask yourself if you're conflicted about being there. Maybe you don't believe you're receiving the recognition you deserve. On the flip side, perhaps you're feeling guilty because they pay you so well and you don't truly believe that you deserve it. Maybe you're not following your heart's desire, or maybe you just need to manage your time more effectively. Explore your thoughts and feelings, and pay attention to the negative self-talk you do all the time. What physical behaviors do you repeat? What spiritual issues are involved? Maybe you just need to go to bed earlier the night before so that you can get up earlier. You might need more time to get ready than you'd like to admit. Maybe you could decide to read the paper after work or on your lunch break. Suddenly, a number of options become available to you and you realize that you get to choose. That's quite empowering. (Old Critical Dragon won't like this one bit and will work harder to test you to see if you mean it when you create a change. Know this and plan accordingly.)

Regret is also a feeling imposed by Critical Dragon. You need compassion and validation for yourself. You can recognize the attitudes of the past, experience some empathy for yourself and make another choice in the present and future. Unrecognized, and therefore, unresolved, grief may accompany some of the decisions made in the past.

Speaking of grief, Elisabeth Kübler-Ross[29] offers her work in the field.

JOURNEY GUIDE

Elisabeth Kübler-Ross
Swiss-born psychiatrist and the author of the groundbreaking book, On Death and Dying, *where she first discussed what's now known as the model of the five stages of grief.*

Kübler-Ross defined the five stages of grief with the acronym DABDA, which stands for Denial, Anger, Bargaining, Depression and Acceptance.

Denial might show up as thoughts such as: *This isn't happening,* or *I/he/she/they don't really feel that way, mean what they said, etc.*

Anger you're most likely familiar with.

Bargaining usually takes the form of sentences that begin with "If only…"

Depression is a feeling of sadness.

Acceptance seems to arrive when those other four have been explored and owned. The process isn't necessarily linear, however, and you may cycle back and forth through all of them many times, including acceptance.

Grief doesn't always involve someone's death, as we tend to think of it. Grief can include the death of an idea, a dream, or a loss in some way. Sometimes there's grief mixed in with pleasure, which can be really confusing. Critical Dragon brings perfectionism to mind. You might feel great about having been the host or hostess of a killer dinner party, however, if it nearly killed you in the process, you might not be feeling all warm and runny inside once the last guest leaves. Serving others at your own expense is where this pattern shows up for many people. Stop before you think you need to, because your gauge may require recalibration.

I understand this one wholeheartedly and preach to you from the pulpit of the reformed. I have a history of addressing every situation, whether a dinner party or the kids' bedtime, with the thought, "How can I make this magical?" Magical, yes. Enchanting, yes. Worth lying in a crumpled heap on the floor at the end of it all? No. Enchantment with balance is the goal. Balance comes from being sure that you are in the mix. It isn't about just making life enchanting for those around you.

STORY: The Enchanted Fourth Birthday Party

My typical scenario from the past went something like this: The theme for my four-year old son's birthday party was moons and stars. I handmade the glittering invitations and matching thank-you notes. On the night before the party I had the great idea to make all of the food into moon and star shapes with a cookie cutter. I cut PB & J sandwiches and cheeses into those shapes. I made the cake and decorated it by painting a Matisse-like sun/moon design in icing. Around midnight, I realized that the birthday boy had nothing special to wear to the party so I tiptoed into his room, selected a royal blue T-shirt and painted a moon and stars on it with glow in the dark paint. That gave me the idea to hang glow in the dark stars around the party site. I thought, "How cool would it be to hang glittery stars from the trees?" Wow, I could do face painting on the kids! I made a sample of moon/star designs from which to choose. Since the paints were already out, I decided to cut out a piece of foam core in the shape of a moon and star through which the children could poke their faces for photos to be put in the frames that we were making as a craft project at the party. How fun, also, to whip up a few starry beanbags from scraps of fabric I had, to throw through the holes when the photos were done.

Meanwhile, I never felt the craziness in that whole scene because it energized me. It was quite enchanting, both in its execution and in its memories as well. However, in between the execution and the memories, came the meltdown. After the adrenaline subsided I just felt like collapsing. I didn't, of course, because there was laundry to do and clean up and dinner to be made, etc. Thank goodness my husband is helpful, but in retrospect, enchantment and balance at that point, would've looked different than the way it happened. In my hindsight scenario, other family and friends could have cleaned up and I would've ordered a pizza for dinner. Those simple changes would've made it enchanting and balanced for me.

Everyone's center is different and it's important to know what yours is and to honor it. This isn't a competition. I'm sure that some of you think I was nuts, while others have told me how much they admired the way I created lasting memories for my children. There were still some who measured themselves against me, saying, "I don't know how you do it! I could never be this creative or have enough energy. I must be an awful parent." I wouldn't let them beat themselves up for not doing it my way. I needed to heal from doing it "my way."

A dear friend of mine said something wonderful to me that changed everything about the way I approached these issues. She said, "Just because you can, doesn't mean you have to." Brilliant, Catherine! Remember those wise words if you are one of those who sets about making life enchanting for others and forgets to include yourself in the reverie. Boundaries are very important. If you know where the line is and you consciously step over it, you're probably also already aware of the consequences.

Dr. O. Carl Simonton[30] helps with shifting our attitudes.

 **JOURNEY GUIDE**

> # O. Carl Simonton
>
> *An internationally acclaimed oncologist, author, lecturer and pioneer in the fight against cancer, promotes health through focus on the connection between mind, body, spirit and emotions.*

Focusing our attention on intentionally shifting our attitudes and beliefs can go a long way toward healing on all of those levels. Following is a brief synopsis of The Ten Tenets of the Simonton Cancer Program:

1. Emotions influence health and recovery from disease, as they're a strong driving force in the immune system and other healing systems.
2. Beliefs and attitudes have an effect on our emotions.
3. We can alter our beliefs and attitudes to increase our health.
4. These things can be taught and learned.
5. We all function as physical, mental, social and spiritual/philosophical beings and our needs must be addressed in the context of our families, community and culture.
6. Harmony is central for a healthy balance in the body, mind, spirit and philosophy of individuals, including relationships with self, family, friends, community, planet and universe.
7. We have genetic and instinctual tendencies and abilities that help us move in the direction of health and harmony.
8. These tendencies can be developed and implemented through methods included in the program.
9. The more they are practiced, proficiency evolves, resulting in improved quality of life, thus, improving health.
10. Fear of death or pain is lessened, freeing the energy to get well and live life more fully in the present.

Dragon Alert!

"Blah, blah, blah," says Critical Dragon. "None of those things will help you and you're a fool to believe that they can." Know that your Internal Enchantress understands that thinking this way is just protection from feelings of hurt and disappointment. Have hope and let yourself believe in miracles. Why shouldn't they happen to you?

Simonton takes into account the individual, as did psychiatrists, Drs. Thomas Holmes and Richard Rahe[31].

JOURNEY GUIDES

Thomas Holmes
Richard Rahe

They examined the effects of stress on people and considered why the response to it was worse for some than for others.

Holmes and Rahe discovered that somewhere between six to eighteen months after a series of events perceived as stressful and anxiety-ridden, illness often occurred. They also observed that the common source for disease, both acute and chronic, was stress.

Two goddesses stride on the path. First, we encounter Suzanne Kobassa[32]

JOURNEY GUIDE

> # Suzanne Kobassa
>
> *Researcher who documented the psychological parameters of health and introduced the term, "hardiness" as a positive influence in healing.*

     Kobassa pinpointed hardiness and broke it down into three main parts: commitment, control and challenge. Commitment addresses feelings toward the self, family, work and social environment. A sense of connectedness and purpose is important. Control refers to power in terms of self-responsibility.

     Critical Dragon breaks the spirit through feelings of alienation, a sense of having no control over events and their effect, as well as negative self-talk that keeps the old patterns intact.

     Next we meet Dr. Christian Northrup, [33] OB/GYN.

JOURNEY GUIDE

> # Christian Northrup
>
> *Possibly American women's most trusted medical adviser and author of several books, including* The Wisdom of Menopause.

     Northrup believes that there's nothing to be gained from perceiving emotions as either good or bad. She prefers to think of them as guidance, and states, "The emotions that feel good are guiding you toward health, while the ones that feel bad are trying to get your attention so that you can change either your perception or your behavior."

     In addressing current knowledge about diet, exercise, medical care, etc., Northrup believes, "the most significant way of contributing to our own good health is through the quality of our thought processes."

     Now here's a woman who possesses a strong Internal Enchantress that hushes Critical Dragon and alters the perceptions of the messages sent and received.

STORY: Unexpected Angel in New York City

I had an enlightening experience while living in New York City that speaks to the value of altering perceptions. One Friday evening, as I walked briskly down Manhattan's sidewalks, I encountered an elderly woman. She had thin, white hair that fell past her shoulders. Her pale scalp was revealed and the Alabaster skin on her arms reflected the light from the street lamp. She sat in a wheelchair, her body twisted and contorted. Her lipstick was fuchsia, but my attention was drawn to her twinkling brown eyes and her wild sense of humor. *How could a woman in her condition be so vibrant?* I wondered.

A native New Yorker, she said in her characteristic dialect, "Dahling, I'm not selling any pencils or anything, but if you'd like to help me, you could give my arms a rest by pushing me a few blocks."

When I asked where she was headed, she told me she was going to synagogue to attend Friday night services. I smiled because that's where I was headed as well; to a synagogue I'd never been to before.

We chatted along the way and, by the time we arrived there, I was convinced that she was leading a blessed life. We sat side-by-side during services and then I offered to assist her with getting home. A wary New Yorker, she shook her head no, regardless of how innocent I looked. Then she added that she'd be happy to be rolled back to her place on the corner in which we had met. As a newly transplanted New Yorker, I understood her fears.

I pushed her wheelchair along the bumpy cracks in the sidewalk. We were about halfway there, when a sudden storm appeared and showered down rain, while the heavens thundered. Startled, I let out a short scream and began sprinting behind her, gripping the handles of her wheelchair.

The rubber on her tires looked dangerously worn and I was afraid of getting fried by lightning. While running, I tried to drape my upper body over her to help keep her dry. Amused by my charade, she cackled and told me to slow down before I got a speeding ticket. She informed me that rain is wet and that it doesn't matter whether you're moving quickly or slowly in it, if you're outside when it's raining, you get wet.

We dissolved in laughter until another clap of thunder sobered us, but only briefly. She said if I were scared I could sit on her lap, but that I might crush her and that would ruin her whole day.

The two of us presented quite a picture, soaked and howling in the rain that had become gentle. I walked slowly again. She told me of her long year in the hospital, several years back, following a sudden illness.

Although she'd been born with a bone deformity, she reported having led a relatively normal life until that year that she became ill. At the hospital, she'd been placed in an interior room, with no windows. She used to annoy the nurses, she said, asking several times a day for the weather report.

In some instances she was not treated very kindly. One nurse snapped at her, saying, "Why are you so concerned with the weather? You're not going anywhere!"

"I go outside in my mind," she replied, and "I'll stay in if the weather is bad."

She shared her realization in that moment, that there is no bad weather. There's just weather, and people decide whether it's good or bad.

A few months later, a kind nurse had her moved to a room with a window. She said she cried with joy each day to see the sun rise and set, to watch the rain come down and the tops of the trees blow in the wind. She vowed that if she ever got out of the hospital, she would love what was given to her each day, beginning with the weather. She couldn't wait to lift her face to the warm sun or have her hair washed in rainwater.

I tilted my head back and let the drops of rain mingle with the tears that washed my face. I've been forever changed by this woman, and told her so that night.

The rain stopped and we arrived at her corner. I looked at the faces of people passing by and wondered if they could see this tiny angel with me, in her big, shiny wheelchair or if they didn't see either of us at all.

We said, "Goodnight," and I returned to my apartment in the area of the city called Hell's Kitchen. It had been a magical evening, in so many ways.

The following Friday night, I looked for her, and for several weeks after that, but I never saw her again. I still feel her spirit, however, as she had became a part of me. And, especially when it rains, I think of her.

Richard Bach[34] wrote in his book, *Illusions*, "Perspective: use it or lose it."

Activities:

Altered Perceptions

1. **Do your laundry.** (If you get nothing else from this exercise you will look nice because you are wearing clean clothes.) Notice your attitude. If your attitude is negative, think about ways you can shift it to be more positive. If you enjoy doing laundry, consider ways to enhance the experience further. Practice the Zen of Laundry.
2. **Recall a time when a major decision was made for you (rather than by you) that affected you deeply. Look at this situation from your present perspective to see what gifts or lessons it brought you.** (This could be a move to another state when you were 12 years old, being fired from a job, etc.) You may see now how the move led to meeting a lifelong friend or the job firing led to a better job with a terrific group of co-workers.
3. **Recall a recent experience that left you with regrets. Shift that perception to become aware of the gifts that also came out of that experience.**
4. **Select a current situation that could use a shift.** It could be a relationship, something job-related or that there are too many papers piled up on your countertop. Close your eyes and breathe possibilities. Let yourself try on all of the options, even those that are absurd. You may stumble upon an idea that had not occurred to you that could shift things, as well as your perception of them.
5. **Consider that you are right where you are supposed to be, doing exactly what you are supposed to be doing in your life, at this very moment.** Let yourself try it on and see how it feels. How are you different from a moment ago, or yesterday, when the SHOULDS were spewing from Critical Dragon's mouth? Responding as if this were already true, how do you look? How do you feel? What do others say about you? What do you say about yourself? What were you glad to have let go of?

Action Plan:

Take stock of your perceptions about major issues, such as politics, religion, money, sex and relationships, for instance. Then move from the global to the specific and notice which perceptions are aligned with who you are (or perceive yourself to be) today. Consider which perceptions you would like to shift to become more aligned with Divine energy, your community, Mother Earth, etc. and the vision of the self you would like to become. Write these down in your journal and become the proud owner of Key #2, the key to unlocking your perceptions.

Chapter Seven: Journaling

<u>**Key #3**</u>

This is a rest stop in which to write, dream, and explore yourself. (Be aware of whose inner voice you're listening to so you don't lose your balance and fall into the pit. Critical Dragon has been known to use voice disguisers and snatch journaling journeyers at this point.)

Thank goodness that Julia Cameron,[35] prolific writer and teacher, is here. She assists us with journaling as a form of meditation.

JOURNEY GUIDE

Julia Cameron

*Journaling lowers stress, alters our brain hemispheres,
allows discovery of an inner contact with a creative source
and gives birth to imaginative insights.*

The Artist's Way is only one of her many popular books. In it, each week of her twelve-week program, offers a specific focus. Each day also includes "Morning Pages, brain drain, true north," and every week, an "Artist's Date."

Morning Pages are three pages of longhand, stream-of-consciousness writing, written upon awakening each day. Different from keeping a diary, which can become a documentation of daily events, Morning Pages allow brain drain, at the start of each day. It rids you of the petty issues and mundane thoughts that intermingle (or "muck up," in Dragon-speak) your deeper issues, dreams and desires. This brain drain clears your path and puts you in touch with your inner power.

Without conscious awareness, we can all wake up with leftovers in our systems. Who wants to carry that spat you had with your spouse, boss, friend, toll booth worker into the digestion of your breakfast? That's the gunk that you'll drain out that had the potential to hang over your day like the dark cloud over Ziggy's head. (Remember the animated character of everything-always-goes-wrong, I-just need-some love, Ziggy? I'm pretty sure he didn't journal.)

The process of finding the "true north," which Cameron believes occurs somewhere around one to one-and-a-half pages into the three written each morning, becomes the focused direction of energy that marches you toward your deepest desires. Chopra, one of our guides from the Mindfulness stop, reminds us that we become what we think about most often. So what happens during this process of finding our true north is that our minds transfer what we're most immediately concerned with to what is deeply significant to our unblocking and growth. It becomes difficult to ignore issues that reoccur on the Pages, again and again This holds true for strengths and skills, as well as weaknesses and blocks. As the obstacles reveal themselves and the desires become clear, the course of your true north is apparent and can be set with intent. Even when there's uncertainty because you may be exploring more than one path, your true north, or intended direction, will make itself known. Most often, action manifests on the page before it's carried out in the physical realm.

Cameron discusses how the logical brain was, and is, the part of the brain in charge of survival. She also refers to the logical brain as the "Censor," and the inventive, creative, "holistic" side of the brain as the "Artist brain." Cameron states that writing the Morning Pages will "allow you to detach from your negative Censor."

Note: "Negative Censor" is another sneaky alias that Critical Dragon uses.

Now for an explanation of the gratifying Artist's Date. It's a weekly assignment to make and keep a date with yourself. The block of time may be two hours or all day, but it becomes a commitment to set aside time to nurture your creative spirit.

According to Cameron, "Doing your Morning Pages, you are sending—notifying yourself and the universe of your dreams, dissatisfactions, hopes. Doing your Artist's Date, you are receiving—opening yourself to insight, inspiration and guidance."

STORY: My Friend, Jackie.

Jaqueline Rector, Ph.D. in Philosophy, and one of my dearest friends, died unexpectedly on December 26, 1997. She was a beautiful, passionate woman and an exquisite writer. She was a writer by profession. Among the many gifts, both tangible and intangible, that she had given me through the years was Cameron's book, *The Artist's Way: A Spiritual Path to Higher Creativity*. I had received it for one of the big birthdays; my fortieth. In it, she had inscribed the words, "The happiest of birthdays and the richest in creativity."

I was nursing our third child, a new baby girl, as I read *The Artist's Way* for the first time. Experiencing the devastating effects of the earthquake that we had survived prior to leaving our home in California earlier that year, becoming pregnant, moving three times, suffering from PTSD (Post-Traumatic Stress Disorder every time a truck rumbled by), giving birth and being sleep deprived, had all taken their toll on my creativity and nearly put to death my ability to write. Gratitude journals took all of the energy for writing that I could muster. Reading the book was delightful. It was just what I needed to reconnect. Although I was excited about the process of writing these Pages, my problem was that I was already waking up too early to someone else's little body alarm. I couldn't get up even earlier, but knew I needed to do the Pages, so I forged ahead. (With all of the changes I had endured when I received this gift, I feared they'd look like "mourning" pages.)

I tried nursing my baby on one side, holding the book on the other and switching every ten minutes. I had difficulty reading, much less writing, with tiny arms and legs flailing. Nursing my baby and writing the Pages each deserved its own special time. Not wanting to disappoint my friend, I made the tiniest journal and wrote very large in order to fill three pages. That lasted about three days. Then I decided I'd get a composition book and only write one page. I explained out loud to Ms. Cameron, (Julia, I like to call her) that I didn't really have the time to do this and that desire could only take me so far, realistically. One page felt like I was cheating. I don't cheat and I don't do things half way. When I realized that I was expending a great deal of energy trying *not* to journal every day, I knew a shift was in order.

I began my writing with how annoyed I was—knowing I'd go the distance---like I always do.

Always. I'd find a way to make it work; find a way to do it all. (I wasn't an enlightened Enchantress yet.) Then I felt guilty, which got explored, too, because Jackie would never want her gift to cause me any internal strife. I was so deeply grateful for her intention, her wisdom of knowing what I needed, whether or not I did, and became hugely aware of the preciousness of true friendship. I was also aware that I was still writing grudgingly. Julia says that's okay. So I wrote some more. My writing unleashed a fairly belligerent tirade about how I didn't want to force myself to do one more thing that was someone else's idea, in the same rigid, disciplined manner that mirrored the process of my life. I discovered that I was mad as hell and not going to take it anymore! That's when I fell in love with the discoveries on the Pages and committed to writing them each morning.

That was startling to me.

The focus of my journal writing switched to my loving and well-meaning family of origin, whom I never wanted to disappoint, and to the discipline and focus they taught me. That's helped me to keep my many plates spinning in the air at all times. But being so industrious and achievement-oriented left me with a play imbalance. It's hard work keeping those plates in the air. The truth is that there have been several times in my life when I wished I could just walk away from some of those mundane responsibilities and play. My children gave me a glorious excuse to do that, guilt-free, but I also needed to play in solitude.

To this day, written in black and white on the journal pages, I'm able to see that, while it serves me well out there in the world to maintain all those plates, it's still a challenge to pay attention to the inner world, when it comes to playing. It's hard to let myself play if all of my cyclical and endless chores have not been completed. (Critical Dragon often gets submerged in bubble bath water while I soothe the fire-breathing burns I sustain regarding this issue.)

And the Artists' Dates! They are the most precious and fun experiences, yet I have traded my soul away to the Lemmejust Dragon. That's the one that hypnotizes me into saying, "Let me just…do a load of wash, chop the vegetables for dinner, vacuum, and *then* I'll paint, go for a walk in the park, star gaze, etc." The Lemmejust Dragon is such a monster. No, rather a teacher who is trying to help me set boundaries for myself that balance responsibilities with creative open space.

Many of the Pages contain apologies to myself for letting other people and situations take me away from these dates. These insights are profound and undeniable when witnessed in writing.

Through journaling, I've reclaimed misplaced parts of myself that hold enchantment. For instance, I recalled the root beer barrel candies of my youth, and was delighted to learn that they can still be found in the grocery store. I can taste my uncomplicated childhood in the root beer flavor, whenever I wish.

Moving into my own imagery with joy, I wrote about new rituals to create with my family. In the winter, the nightly ritual of taking tea up to my bedside table in my grandmother's antique silver tea service is delicious. In the summer, the tea is replaced with water upon which floats lemon slices or mint from the garden.

Whether I had ever written one paragraph or had never opened the book, mattered not at all to my friend, Jackie. She would've loved me just the same. The Pages, though, mattered to me. They still do. I write them each morning just the way I wash my face and brush my teeth.

Pearlin and Schooler, who already taught us something about stress and self concept, suggest that for a week or so, a daily journal should be kept, to record the critical and negative messages to the self. (Critical Dragon would feel so flattered to star on the pages.) The current mood is recorded, as well as internal struggles or conflicts that come into awareness, either before or after the negative thoughts. One week later, you get to look back at the writings to see if any patterns have emerged. If so, see if the patterns reflect self-esteem issues with regard to your body, personal appearance, personality, interpersonal relationships, or work. Then observe mood changes or changes in daily stress. Consider whether these stressors presented themselves before or after the negative thoughts. Deciphering patterns may provide clues to dealing with stress and moods as they shift with daily life.

How exciting! A whole slew of creative, intelligent writers are gathered at this spot. There's Natalie Goldberg,[36] as well as Anne Lamott,[37] Barbara Ganim and Susan Fox.[38]

JOURNEY GUIDE

Natalie Goldberg

A passionate poet, teacher, writer and artist who encourages others to paint strong images with words that resonate deeply within the heart and soul. Among other books, Goldberg wrote the pioneering book, Writing Down the Bones, Freeing the Writer Within, *that explores writing as a Zen practice.*

JOURNEY GUIDE

Anne Lamott

The author of several novels and works of non-fiction that are mostly biographical. She has a sharp wit and a father, Kenneth Lamott, who was a writer as well. Her book, Bird by Bird *was also done as a documentary film:* Bird by Bird: A Film Portrait of Writer Anne Lamott.

JOURNEY GUIDE

Barbara Ganim & Susan Fox

Artists and writers of the workbook, Visual Journaling, Going Deeper Than Words, *who believe that visual journaling provides a framework in which the self can, literally, be drawn outward.*

Writing is not the only form of journaling. Art journals offer a non-verbal path back to the self. Images can appear on the page that you're not aware of having created. Ganim and Fox's workbook offers a six-week program that contains exercises geared toward "using art to reduce stress, release anger, resolve conflicts, get in touch with feelings and give voice to your soul, even if you can't draw."

Ganim and Fox suggest that visual journaling is a healing therapy for people who may be suffering from illness or disease. Since stress has been shown to cause "immune system dysfunction, cellular abnormality and the eventual degeneration of body systems," visual journaling is helpful because it aids with the release of stress.

There are four basic steps in the process of visual journaling. They are: 1) Setting a Clear Intention, 2) Quieting the Mind through Body-Centered Awareness, 3) Seeing with Your Inner Eye through Guided Visualization, and 4) Drawing Your Inner Images.

The preparation for this journey may be as healing as the journey itself. Setting the intention brings focus to what is seeking expression. Quieting the mind brings awareness to the thoughts, feelings, and physical body, in the present moment. Body-centered awareness is a technique that shifts the attention from the mind to a specific part of the body and the breath. From there, attention is drawn to a part of the body that requires it. This begins the process of movement from outer to inner vision. You might imagine what the feeling or sensation chosen to be expressed looks like, visually, when seeing it with the inner eye. Inner images are recorded in drawings, rather than words, and include all of the feelings or sensations seen in the mind's eye in the previous step. This process becomes an imagery-rich recording of the daily meditations experienced.

A college student who had been on an Enchanted Journey tour stated that she enjoyed the process of creating a special journal but found that actually writing in it daily was quite tedious, given all of the writing assignments required of her for school. She remembered that she could do visual journaling as an option to writing words. She was thrilled to be able to doodle in her journal, using symbols that reflected her moods and issues. She said journaling that way held an added bonus because her curious roommates wouldn't understand her musings if they violated her privacy and read her journal.

The great artist Pablo Picasso said, "Painting is just another way of keeping a diary."

Anne Frank, [39] a courageous young woman whose diary became famous through the efforts of her father, Otto Frank, joins us.

JOURNEY GUIDE

Anne Frank

In Anne Frank: The Diary of a Young Girl, *journal entries were written to an imaginary friend, recording the details of her experiences and times, while being hidden away from the Nazis. The journal became not only a focus for the life of her spirit, but a legacy as well.*

Whether you choose to journal with or without words, selecting or making a journal, choosing a writing instrument or gathering art supplies, deciding which music or environmental sounds to play while journaling, all add to the experience.

Of course, I'm here to invite you not to get too caught up in this preparation process. Critical Dragon can develop what I call the "Ed Norton Syndrome." I made this syndrome up, based on Art Carney's portrayal of Ed Norton, in the 1950's show, "The Honeymooners."

Jackie Gleason played the character of Ralph Kramden, Ed Norton's best friend and star of the show. He'd become annoyed with Ed when he attempted to write a short note or letter. Ed would have to set the conditions before putting pen to paper. He'd sweep the table, grandly, with his arm, to clear the already empty space. Then he'd extend his arms and hold them in a relaxed posture. The process would be repeated, this time, repositioning the sleeve on his arm. He did this again and again, each time touching the pen to paper but not writing a single word, until Ralph would blow up, unable to stand the procrastination for another moment and scream at him. He must've recognized the voices of both of their Critical Dragons.

If you notice yourself getting bogged down in the process of selecting a journal, a pen, a time to write, etc. sit down and write about it with the nearest pencil, on a napkin, if necessary. Just get it out of you.

In addition to my day job as an Enchantress, I'm also of service as a psychotherapist. Journaling has a powerful clinical application as well. I encourage some clients to keep Dragon journals. You might want to do that. Through these journals, you may become aware of the Dragon's chatter to which you've responded unconsciously. You could have one journal and only write about the Dragon when it's in your face or you may pick a day of the week to take Dragon Inventory.

Like Neale Donald Walsch's, *Conversations With God* books, you may find yourself writing your own conversations with God. Maybe you'll want to write to people, living or dead, with whom you have unfinished business. Writing to them can release pent-up emotions and bring a sense of peace and closure. Many times when letters to the living are written, they're not sent. The exercise allows expression and isn't necessarily a step toward sharing your feelings with them.

People have experienced automatic writing. Their pens move effortlessly across the page, recording wisdom that they didn't know they had. Try it. Quiet yourself and put pen to paper and see what happens.

Journals can also be used to focus on specific issues that you're wishing to heal. Some become safe "rooms" for survivors of abuse.

STORY: The Room with Many Doors

I'm reminded of the power of journaling as a healing tool when I recall a client that I saw years ago. She had worked hard in therapy with other well-trained therapists, before coming to me. She's a survivor of sexual abuse within her nuclear family and had learned to understand herself, divorce herself from her abusive family members, grieve, heal and create a new, loving and supportive family of her own. She was, however, still plagued with nightmares. She came to me to assist her with making the unconscious material, conscious.

In combination with some hypnotherapy to retrain her responses to feeling out of control, I offered her the tool of journaling. She found it to be most effective in calming her and directing her focus. It was sometimes difficult for her to practice self-hypnosis while in crisis mode, even with the aid of an audiocassette. It required too much energy for her to be still and calm.

The journal, however, became a place to discharge the energy through her pen. That offered her a sense of freedom as she chose to write with black or red markers when addressing her perpetrators, or blue to calm her inner child. She felt empowered by the decision to write very large, with flourishes, expletives, or exclamation points. She'd write their names and/or what they had done to her and tear the pages from the journal. Sometimes she destroyed the pages by burning them in the fireplace. When paper shredders became household conveniences, she was thrilled. Shredding, bagging, and recycling were a favorite pastime. The activity was akin to Wilbur's notion of inclusion, transcendence and transformation.

During sessions, I observed her creativity and empowerment. I'd hand her a pad and pen and tell her to rewrite the ending to a disturbing dream or to an actual event. Her hand was a blur as she crossed "T"s with the motion of a swordswoman. "I"s were dotted with what appeared to be the point of a dagger piercing the page. At completion, she'd exhale a great gust of breath that had held the stress of the world inside of her. Silent for a moment or two afterward, a smile would slowly creep across her face and she'd ask, "Want to know what I wrote?" I, of course, always did.

Together we created an exercise for her to do when she had the reoccurring nightmare we came to call: The Room with Many Doors. She'd find herself trapped in a room with many doors, with one or more of her perpetrators. After an exhausting struggle, she'd finally break free, but no matter which door she chose, she'd be led right back into the room. There was never any escape. Night after night, she'd experience the dream in which she was breathless and trying to scream. Only silent, strained whispers struggled to eek out sound, often leaving her throat sore and voice hoarse for the rest of the day. The dream usually resulted in a full-blown panic attack and the loss of an entire night's sleep.

In the journaling exercise, upon awakening from the dream, she'd grab the bedside pad and marker and draw another door, one that did, in fact, lead to a safe room. In that room she could meet her Internal Enchantress who would bear witness to her fears and offer her safety and security. That room, through our design, had an outside passageway. She could go through that door and never return because she had with her everything that she needed. Eventually, after having written and drawn out the solution a number of times, she began to be able to create the door, the safe room and the way out, while she was dreaming. At last contact with her, she reported rarely experiencing the dream anymore.

STORY: We'll Love You If You're Thin

Another client who benefited from journaling came in with issues of isolation and discovered much more. She was an assertive, take-charge woman in the corporate world, who saw herself as a "little, fat, whiny girl" in her internal world. She felt as if she were masquerading at the office; convinced that it was only a matter of time before her colleagues would see through her. Humor was used to hide her true feelings.

I suggested journaling.

We discussed whether she'd like to write to her fat self, her skinny self, God, to the others present in her life or all of the above. She often wrote to everyone, including people she didn't know that she imagined judged her by her physical appearance. Mostly, however, she chose to write to a gentle and benign God who could love her fat, love her when she was whining and even though she was not perfect.

After a few sessions, we uncovered her inner child's history of believing that she could only be loved if she were "good," meaning that she went along with what other people wanted. That's often a set-up for sexual abuse to occur. I asked if her physical boundaries had even been violated, and she confirmed that they had, although not by any relatives. In her family, however, being "good" meant being thin and in control. She was expected not to give in to impulses, desires, or emotions. Throwing her head back in laughter she said, "Now you can understand why I'm fat, alone, and only God Almighty Himself could possibly love me." Just as quickly, she burst into wracking sobs. Through her tears she judged herself, as her family always had, for "being out of control."

Her journal exercise for that week was to observe her self-judgments that were carryovers from her family's judgments. She enjoyed journaling. It provided her with much needed freedom to express herself and she got in touch with her anger toward her family. Confining her feelings to the pages created boundaries that were safe.

Later, her writing began to focus on forgiving them. In her case, it was clear that her family acted without malice or awareness of their own wounds. They believed that being good, thin, and in control were keys to happiness and acceptance from others. She was able to see how she had taken the reins with regard to judging herself. There was the discovery of resentment that she'd need to be those things in order to be loved. The unconscious answer came as a rebellion that said, "If you *really* love me, you'll love me bad, fat, and emotional." She said that two of those she could still hide from her colleagues, but not her weight. Her journaling shifted toward nurturing her inner child and building a solid foundation in which she could experience self-love. She has done a remarkable job.

Journaling is a terrific tool because anywhere, anytime, there is usually a pen and paper somewhere within arm's reach, especially in the middle of the night, when other people are less likely to be available to talk. More and more people blog now. Expression by means of an electronic device and through both hands is different, I believe, than it is through either pen and paper and your dominant hand or art.

Activities:
Journaling
1. **What is the best part of each day? What are the reasons?**
2. **What is the worst, or most challenging, part of the day? What are the reasons? What would you like to change about this?**
3. **Make a list of stressful or anxiety-producing experiences you've had in the last month. Put a little dot by those which are on-going sources of stress.**
4. **List twenty sources of stress for you.** (Your Critical Dragon is ecstatic right now because you're focusing on the negative stuff and, even though you say your life is stressful, you may not be able to write down more than six things at first, which will also delight your Dragon!)
5. **List twenty things that bring you joy.** (These become your Stress Busters.) Even if you haven't done these things for a long time, it doesn't matter. List them. Now, notice which ones serve you in a healthy way for mind, body, spirit and emotions. Place a line through the ones that don't and replace them with ones that do. Do not be surprised if some of the things that bring you joy also bring you stress.

Let me break from format here (spontaneity is part of the enchantment!) and share a story before you arrive at your Action Plan.

STORY: These Were the Best of Times/the Worst of Times

I recall another college student tour, during which one tourist, upon completion of these activities, realized that her most stressful time of day was late afternoon. That's when she rushed home from school and tried to organize dinner before her children came home on the bus. She made a new plan to use both the drive home, and the forty-five minutes she had before the kids arrived, to nurture herself. She recognized that dinner would still get made, but that time for herself was what always got shoved aside.

Another young man stated that his worst time of day was the morning. He habitually wasted time rifling through his scattered papers because he had studied too late the night before, fallen into bed and awakened exhausted and unorganized. This set the tone for his whole day. After further discussion, I suggested that he set a bedtime for himself that allowed ten to fifteen minutes of transition time to unwind first, to select his clothes the night before, pack his lunch and organize his schoolwork. He laughed, as he recalled his mother doing that for him when he was small. He said he would feel like his own "little mommy" and that it felt good. He was willing to try that change, and said that if he were only able to do it half of the time it would be a huge improvement.

The exercise that asks you to list twenty sources of stress, as well as the one that asks you to list twenty sources of joy, both brought big groans from Critical Dragons. We discovered that listing the sources of stress was stressful, as was crossing out the stress busters that were detrimental to body, mind, spirit and emotions.

Several attendees noted smoking and alcohol consumption as chosen stress-reducing activities. Their Critical Dragons went berserk when they were told they would need to replace those harmful activities with suggestions for healthier ones. Each person was asked to share, aloud, his or her list of stress busters. People were very enthusiastic and either confirmed an item on their list, or hurried to add ones they had forgotten. They were instructed to post their list in a prominent place in their homes, and refer to it often, as well as to continue adding to the list.

It was revealed that what one person had on the list as a stressor, another may have had on the list as a stress buster. Sex, shopping and sports seem to have created the biggest controversy. One woman yelled out, "Sex is a stress-buster!" Immediately, two other women commented that they had left sex off of their stress-inducing list. This prompted another woman to call out that shopping was orgasmic for her. A man replied with, "Shopping! How did I leave this off of my list of stress-inducers?" He went on to say that his wife shared the viewpoint of the orgasmic shopper. This awareness became grist for the mill in discussing how the couple may decide to spend their free weekend time. It was definitely an opportunity to celebrate both the uniqueness and the unity among the tourists.

Action Plan:

    A. Focus on what elements or qualities help to create the best time of day and invite them to other parts of your day.

    B. Remember what you discovered about your worst time of day and work toward eliminating or changing those stressors.

    C. Journal about those stressors on your list and consider various options to change your perception about them.

    D. Journal about how you learned to cope with your stress. (Do you drink after dinner like your father did? Do you ignore it and get busy like Mom used to do?) Consider that you have a choice that needs to involve acknowledgement of an issue and then a healthy means with which to address it.

    E. Write your Morning Pages.

    F. Pat yourself on the back for owning three keys already.

Chapter Eight: Sensory Experiences

Stop here to encounter the sights, sounds, smells, tastes and textures along the way. The lovely author, Diane Ackerman,[40] writes about the importance of experiencing the world through the senses.

JOURNEY GUIDE

Diane Ackerman

Paints pictures with her words as she describes the world as a "sense-luscious" place in her book, A Natural History of the Senses.

Ackerman further supports the importance of the senses as tools that bring enrichment to life. She refers to Helen Keller as "one of the greatest sensuists of all time," and says about her:

Blind, deaf, mute, Helen Keller's remaining senses were so finely attuned that when she put her hands on the radio to enjoy music, she could tell the difference between the cornets and the strings. She listened to the colorful, down-home stories of life surging along the Mississippi from the lips of her friend Mark Twain. She wrote at length about the whelm of life's aromas, tastes, touches, feelings, which she explored with the voluptuousness of a courtesan. Despite her handicaps, she was more robustly alive than many people of her generation.

Our friend, Perls, believed that neurotic behavior stemmed from the inability to see the obvious, which led him to encourage others to lose their minds in order to be able to come to their senses. Connecting to your senses and to yourself can move you to feelings of aliveness. Your senses are pathways to mindfulness that activate the present awareness. You must then make the awareness conscious.

The astounding Ashley Montagu,[41] psychologist and anthropologist, educator, lecturer and author is here.

JOURNEY GUIDE

Ashley Montagu

Most well-known for his extensive study on connection through the sense of touch. He focused on the element of love and also racial and sexual equality.

Senses are used to communicate with one another. Physical touch is one source of connection. Montagu examined the critical importance of touch and its relationship to physical and psychological well-being.

I had the privilege of attending a workshop in which Montagu was the facilitator. He had us select a partner whom we'd never met, and sit on the floor opposite him or her. Then we were instructed to take turns and trace the face of the other with our fingers. It was a deeply intimate and emotional experience for us, evoking a variety of feelings, and awakening us to the importance of this sense.

Kabat-Zinn suggests that touch is not the only significant sense. There are many other ways to connect, as well. He states:

We make contact with each other and connect through all of our senses, with our eyes, our ears, our noses, our tongues, our bodies, and our minds. These are our doors of connection to each other and to the world. They can hold extraordinary meaning when the contact is made with awareness rather than out of habit.

Fully experiencing the senses can connect us with our own histories and our deepest selves. Have you ever walked into an environment in which you were suddenly transported by the scent? You can be moved to another time and place, before there's conscious awareness of what that sense memory is linked to for you.

STORY: The Hardware Store of My Childhood

Several years ago, we were on a family vacation on Hilton Head Island, South Carolina. There was a long wait at a local restaurant. Frustrated and hungry, we left our name and wandered into a nearby hardware store to help pass the time. Upon entering, I felt a wave of wonder and anticipation. Suddenly, my eyes flooded with tears.

My children asked, "What's wrong, Mommy? What happened?"

I choked out the meaningless words, "childhood hardware store smell."

They probably thought it was low blood sugar or that I'd been out in the sun too long, when my husband came bounding up from the back of the store excitedly yelling, "This hardware store smell is unbelievable! It takes me right back to being a kid in Philadelphia."

I grew up in Miami, Florida, so we certainly didn't frequent the same stores, yet the scent triggered intense feelings, and then memories, for each of us. I'm sure there wasn't "Essence of Childhood Hardware Store" in a room deodorizer. The original smell was undoubtedly a combination of pesticides, mold and other deadly, toxic chemicals crammed into a small and, often, too-hot, space.

Why, for me, did that also bring tears? I realized that, in that instant, I had returned to the hardware store of my childhood with my dad. He had died a number of years ago, when I was only twenty-two, but I had been transported by that smell to the age of four, to a place that smelled the same, and in which they knew my daddy by name.

I had felt the stiffness of my brand new jeans; first-time jeans for a tiny girl's premiere trip to the hardware store. I'd only worn and loved girly dresses until that day. My rite of passage meant that, not only was I old enough to go there with Daddy, as each of my older siblings had, but that my parents were sure that I, unlike my sister, wouldn't eat any nails if no one were looking.

The smell of the sweat of hard labor had been in the crease of my daddy's elbow. I had held his arm tightly, poking, pressing and releasing the vein on the back of his strong hand with my finger, to stop and release his blood flow.

Although I didn't have the words to express it, I believe that the hardware store held the possibility of creation for my daddy, in the same way that a blank sheet of forty-pound weight watercolor paper and paints hold that for me today. I could smell the power of that.

Daddy bought charcoal for the barbeque grill there and I could inhale the whole experience of Sundays with my family; *the going to the beach, coming home, washing the gritty sand away in a tub of Mr. Bubble, Daddy standing on the freshly-mowed grass grilling my favorite hotdogs, with roasted marshmallows for dessert* (only if I finished my meal).

He got the gasoline for our mower at the hardware store of my childhood, too. The wet tears on my face were my unconscious testimony to missing him.

They were also the vehicle for the lesson in altering perceptions, the next time there's a long wait at a restaurant.

STORY: A Memory Scent and Received

As I write about the sense of smell, I recall work with a client who was in her forties when she came to me. She wanted to connect with the memories of her mother, who had been killed in a car accident when the client was only four years old. She was with a babysitter and waited for her mother to return from shopping.

We did hypnotherapy to recall the daily routines that she either observed or shared with her mother. First, she remembered watching her mother comb her auburn hair. The "fancy" brush was silver and her mother tilted her head to the side as she moved the brush through it.

Inviting other sense memories evoked the recollection of her favorite meal as a young child. It was macaroni and cheese and she remembered it being made, especially for her, on her birthday. She sat in the hypnotherapy chair, eyes closed, a smile spread across her face, as she delighted in seeing the cheese stretch above the bowl and smelling the aromas in the kitchen. I asked her to lean in and smell her mother's scent. She was moved to tears as she inhaled deeply and slowly.

Following the trance work, I asked if it were her natural scent or if a particular perfume or powder added a layer of memory. She said that there was a distinct perfume, but that she could not identify it. I suggested that she go to the fragrance counter at a department store and begin her search, also inquiring about which fragrances might have been popular in the years that she was a young child.

The following week she reported having smelled several fragrances that did not recreate that distinctive scent. She said she'd been afraid of forgetting the exact scent and that it would get lost in the blending of fragrances if she were to find it. Then she went to a perfumery; a store selling only perfume, with knowledgeable salespeople. After smelling a handful of fragrances that she learned were popular at the time, she smelled it, her mother's scent, and was overwhelmed with emotion.

Weeping, with opened connections of love, lost from her past, she bought two bottles of the perfume. She keeps it on her dresser and starts her day by closing her eyes and opening the bottle of perfume that has evoked several other forgotten memories. For many years, the only recollections she had of her mother were of the day that Mommy never came back from the store. Stories were told to her but she didn't have her own recall. These memories are her own and, through them, she has recaptured a missing part of herself.

STORY: A Comforting Hand

Another client of mine had lost both of his parents within a few years of each other, when he was a young teenager. Although he first sought help thirty years later, his wounds were just beneath the surface. He was deeply saddened by the loss he had experienced when they died.

Crying through the hypnotherapy session, with a depth of sadness that was heart wrenching, he recalled the comfort of his mother's hand on his belly, as a child, when he lay in bed at night. During one session, while he stretched out on his back on the sofa, sobbing, I silently moved to him and gently placed his own hand on his stomach. With eyes still closed, he calmed. His tense muscles relaxed and his breathing deepened and became rhythmic. He smiled through his tears and whispered, "We've tapped into something."

An experiment had begun to see if he could close his eyes and place his hand on his belly any time he needed comforting. It was successful, having incorporated that memory of touch into his healing.

I recall the words of the famous artist, Paul Gauguin. He said, "I shut my eyes in order to see."

What a fitting time for Thomas Moore[42] to be present. Writer, lecturer, and former monk, Moore teaches others how to live life more soulfully. He's been an inspiration.

JOURNEY GUIDE

Thomas Moore

Supports the notion that events deeply rooted in sensory and soulful experience create a fulfilling depth in life. Author of
The Re-enchantment of Everyday Life.

Enchantment is described by Moore as "a spell that comes over us, an aura of fantasy and emotion that can settle in the heart and either disturb it or send it into rapture and reverie." He also states:

A word, a gesture, or an image may be more powerful than a reasoned argument, a ritual or a ceremony more beneficial for human community than any machine or technical development. Becoming a person of deeply grounded and rich imagination may be more desirable than being healthy, politically savvy, or well informed.

Moore points out the difficulty in inviting enchantment to a "disenchanted society," aware of the complaints of modern times that include the high rate of divorce, families separated, lack of community, and nature dishonored. He views these issues as problems with "eros—love and attachment." If the world were viewed as an enchanted place, there would be a move toward intimacy, closeness and connection with one another and nature itself. Moore believes that "Enchantment is both a dulling of the mind and a sharpening of perception."

Roberto Assagioli,[43] Italian psychiatrist and founder of the psychological movement known as *psychosynthesis,* speaks to us.

JOURNEY GUIDE

Roberto Assagioli

Envisioned an approach to human beings that addressed growth as a self-actualized individual with a personality, in addition to transpersonal development of the intuitive, creative and spiritual sides.

Psychosynthesis is a forerunner of the humanistic psychology movement and includes contact and response with one's deepest callings and directions in life. Thoughts of transcendence through beauty speak to the notion of enchantment. The "will to beauty," as eloquently put by Assagioli, is divided into two aspects, "the *contemplation* of beauty and the *creation* of beauty. It is in the creation of beauty, however, that the *will* is more manifest." This addresses the passion of the soul that's moved to action. It's the side-stepping of the personality to the higher or deeper urge to create, to will the creation of beauty or enchantment. This brings depth of meaning to life itself.

The will to create beauty or enchantment can be applied to a simple bath. Many of us bathe children more often than we bathe ourselves. The efficient and perfunctory shower has replaced most of the lingering bath rituals for adults.

I remember when my babies were small, I'd put them in the crib and then run into the shower; leaving one leg out of the stall shower, in case I had to run to them. When it was their bath time, however, I'd gently slide them into the warm water, use natural products to cleanse and soothe them, and follow it with a lavender massage before scooping them up in a cushy towel.

Only a handful of adults, who live the lifestyles of the rich and famous, lounge in a champagne bubble bath while being fanned and fed fresh grapes. Well guess what? The mundane experience of cleansing the body can become an exercise in the creation of enchantment. (Using the "gray water" from the tub afterward to water your plants is environmentally sound and makes them very happy also.)

Here is the main ingredient in a basic recipe for making a warm, relaxing bath, enchanting: Invite all of your senses.

Begin with the sense of sight. If you have a window, position yourself where you can view the sky, moon or trees. If there are no windows, then flowers, artwork or eye-pleasing accessories can help to create aesthetic beauty.

Sound is next. Include birdsong, tree frogs, and various sounds from nature, either present or recorded. Restful music is an option.

The sense of smell can be heightened with aromatherapy oils, bath salts, scented candles, incense, fresh herbs or potpourri.

Taste, usually the least considered sense associated with the bath, can also be introduced. Prepare a bowl of strawberries or a pear. Take it to the next level by drizzling the fruit with chocolate. This provides a snack, while offering a true experience of decadence.

Then there is the sense of touch. Notice the textural contrasts, such as hard surface of the tub and the soft, foamy bubbles. Consider the plush feel of the towels. Indulge in higher thread count towels and sheets. (Don't listen to screaming from Critical Dragon.) This is a place to splurge because they're not purchases you make every week. Good towels and sheets are an investment. They not only enhance the experience of bathing and sleeping, but for a longer period of time than cheaper ones. Towels in the eighty-percent-off bin are usually hideous colors, they ravel horribly, and become car rags within a month or two.

As you play with making your life more and more enchanting, you can explore the continuum of experiences that range from monetary purchases to those that don't add any additional cost. For example, you can purchase a heating element for your towels or place them in the dryer, just prior to the bath. Spending money is not the object; it's using your imagination. Much of the enchantment is in the creation and ingenuity used to heighten every experience.

We all need to realize that we have the power to create enchantment every day. It's neither realistic, nor fair, to think that we only have one shot at enchantment, for one week each year, and that we have to go to Bermuda to get it. We have the ability to heighten our senses and recreate joy every day, right in our own backyards.

For instance, consider what enchants you about a four-star hotel bathroom. (And you don't even have to have ever been in one.) If it's a hanging bathrobe near the tub, buy a hook and hang your bathrobe. Enchantment for $1.19 isn't bad. Buy or make a padded hanger to intensify the feeling of luxury. If you've collected little soaps and lotions from your trips display them, with rolled up washcloths, and fashion magazines, in baskets. Get ocean scented potpourri during the summer and pine scent in the winter. Put a coffee maker in the bathroom, if you wish. Keep an ice bucket on the vanity. Whatever it takes. It's fun to consider how outrageous your ideas can be. Who says that you can't put them into action?

Look at all the ways in which you just expanded your thinking about enchantment and heightening the senses, and we haven't even gone out of the bathroom yet. Imagine the possibilities that lie ahead.

From the bath to the bedroom, enchantment awaits. Case in point; I love to sleep outside, *but* I have too many conditions to make it happen all of the time. Some of them include the weather, the fact that I love critters, but don't want them smelling me or sneaking up on me while I'm asleep and, with the unfortunate state of the world today, there are safety issues to consider. Instead of just feeling sad about my self-imposed limitations, the family sleeps outside, together, on the screened-in porch. We used to do this at the change of every season and several times each summer.

Just like the four-star hotel bathroom, I considered what I love about sleeping outside and decided to decorate our bedroom with the elements that I find most pleasing. Our bedroom set was already made of split pine, but I'd never before made the association between the bedroom furniture we'd purchased years ago and my fantasy to sleep in a cabin in the woods (that happens to have a four-star bathroom.)

Our comforter is reversible, with leaves on one side and roses on the other. It gets flipped during spring and autumn.

I'm tickled to see Guides from all areas of wisdom. Christopher Lowell[44] leaps out from behind a tree trunk.

JOURNEY GUIDE

Christopher Lowell

Visionary designer and celebrity, who utilizes his Seven Layers of Design, which appeal to all of the senses. His motto is "You can do it!"

Lowell was my imaginary cheerleader as I boldly painted our inset ceiling over the bed, a majestic midnight blue. Then I referenced an astronomy chart to add a few specific constellations. Glow in the dark stars created the illusion, along with nightglow paint, for stars appearing further away from my pillow. The walls got two coats of lavender and silk trees were purchased to complete the outdoor feel. I brought a diffuser into the bedroom to layer lavender into the air. It's fun to vary the aromatherapy scent that wafts through the room.

Our middle child is the one who was always overheated, with pink, sweaty cheeks as a kid. He wished for snow, although we didn't live in a location that got any. But a little paint transformed his room into a North Woods lodge. I painted snow-covered mountains, with deep blue night sky and also placed some glow in the dark, stars and a moon in his room. In early January, I bought sale priced half Spruce trees that had been used as Christmas wall hangings, to line the wall by his bed. Trees were painted on the wall in between, for dimension. Upon the trees I hung scented pinecones and realistic-looking birds. My son requested a moose that I painted with a stencil, on the opposite wall. We found a photograph of a real Alaskan moose at an art festival and added that to his room. On his lamp's shade I drew stars and poked pinholes around the outline of each star, through which the light shone.

Each of the girls had her own enchanted room. One was pink and blue with a Victorian cottage garden theme, complete with rosebud and moss topiaries, window boxes and fairies, and the other was gold and pink, with ribbons, angels and antique dolls.

Thomas Moore hadn't seen our rooms and yet he eloquently summed up the experience of our creation when he wrote, "There is no essential conflict between enchanted living and practical, productive activity; they can serve each other: one delighting the spirit of ambition, the other comforting the heart."

Now that we've covered sensory expression in the bathroom and bedrooms, why not invite enchantment to the kitchen? It's so simple. Throw a mandarin orange tea bag into the water steaming your carrots and suddenly you have enchanted carrots. Celestial Seasonings, a well-known tea company, offers terrific recipes for other ways to use their teas. I've added them in the tub, made potpourri with them, as well as in many delicious food recipes. Raspberry Zinger tea bags, soaked in vinegar, make a terrific raspberry vinaigrette dressing. Remember how enchanting those peanut butter and jelly sandwiches cut into shapes with cookie cutters were? The shapes can coincide with the seasons or special holidays. So whether it's in the preparation of meals, creating your environment, or fluffing your spirit, I invite you to play with this idea of adding enchantment. Tempt the senses and see what unfolds...

Activities:

Sensory Experiences

1. **Select an activity (that is healthy for body, mind, and spirit) that you already love, such as gardening, reading, or basketball. Play with the idea of how you can heighten the experience further, or extend the enjoyment.** For example, plant mint in a container near the basketball hoop where you might brush past it. The mint will release its fragrance and also offer a fresh taste if you pull off a leaf and chew on it. (Be sure your plant has not been sprayed with pesticides.)

   If it's winter and you're unable to garden because it is too cold, gather your spring gardening magazines, before recycling them, or order seed catalogs and snip out photographs to paste on to paper to create a garden plan. Mount this on a science board or foam core board and place it somewhere that you'll see it each day. Or, create ways to decorate the winter landscape with statues, bird feeders or other craft projects you can find on-line. If you love to read, make a special bookmark for yourself by laminating photos, collage-style, on to a cardboard strip.

2. **Now select an activity that you perform regularly that is NOT among your list of favorites. Play with ideas to enhance and enchant the activity.**

3. **Select a meal to enhance.** (This may just entail adding a sprig of parsley or a shake of cinnamon to your blob of applesauce.) Go through the checklist to add visual appeal, auditory enhancement (like the addition of music or crunchiness), a pleasing scent, taste and varying textures. In the fall and winter, I often simmer a small one-quart pot of water that contains cloves and cinnamon to

scent the air. In the summer, fresh lemons or the herbs sage or basil are very fragrant. Even just heightening one of the senses can enchant a meal but since it's so fun to play with, why not try to intensify them all?

4. **Do something special for yourself that you would not normally do. Use the checklist again.** Make it easy, like setting a fancy placemat for your breakfast or serving yourself a meal in bed. Add a flower in a vase and a favorite magazine. Try a new tea or coffee blend. Treat yourself like the best guest at your home.

5. **Take a hike.** Literally. It can be a walk around your block but spend some time receiving through each of the senses.

Action Plan:

Continue to play with enhancing experiences you already enjoy and find ways in which to perk up the necessary tasks. Notice which senses you tend to ignore and include them, while augmenting the ones that you already know bring you pleasure and enchantment. Now with four keys in your possession, keep moving forward!

Chapter Nine: Reduced Clutter

Key #5

Now as we journey to the next gate to receive Key #5, you'll notice how much more alive and aware you are of the sensory experiences all around you.

Don't trip over anything on the path. Clutter can exist on the emotional, mental and spiritual planes, as well as on the physical plane. Critical Dragon is delighted with clutter. C.D. can fill a whole room and then live there, unseen.

Emotional issues can be accumulated and dragged from relationship to relationship without ever being sorted through and eliminated. That becomes emotional clutter, often referred to as baggage.

Mental clutter usually takes the form of disorganization that results in missed appointments, inability to focus and overwhelm. Those Critical Dragon negative thoughts that play in an endless repeat cycle in your head are also mental clutter. Thinking that is only about you and how you're alone in everything, detached from your Divine Source, Angels, Higher Self, and your Internal Enchantress, is spiritual clutter. Spiritual clutter may present itself most clearly as a conflict between your tribal family's values of religion and spirituality vs. your own beliefs and practices.

Fairy Stress-sorter, Julie Morgenstern, whom you met while training to receive your Mindfulness key, considers how clutter in all of these realms affects clutter in the physical realm. This is where we're most likely to finally recognize it. Clutter, for most people, is stressful.

Morgenstern advocates written assessments (journaling opportunity) that determine which factors allow the clutter to accumulate in the first place. I had never thought about that prior to reading her book. I've always viewed the phenomenon of the appearance of clutter with the same shock that I view the Sock Monster. I never see it creeping in until it has arrived and taken over the place. Clutter: not there and then there. (It's the opposite with the socks.)

The process of accumulating and clearing clutter occurs in levels. Morgenstern helps with sorting through the obstacles to organization. I encourage you to read her books. For the purpose of clearing clutter and understanding how it gets there in the first place, Morgenstern's *Organizing from the Inside Out: The Foolproof System for Organizing Your Home, Your Office and Your Life,* is invaluable.

My mom comes to mind when I consider the stress I experience if my home environment, including my car, is not neat. When I was growing up in my mom's and dad's house, it was always neat. Of course my dad used to wake us up in the middle of the night to come out to the living room and pick up our shoes, if we had inadvertently left them there. I think I had to do that, let me see, once. Maybe there would be a few bills or a newspaper on the table but Mom would have it swooped up and out of sight by the time unannounced guests stepped out of their cars. I want to be like that when I grow up. I feel calm and comfortable when my environment looks like that. It feels like home. Our kids are still in process with learning this lesson.

Clients always come into my office and comment about how neat, restful and organized it always is. Ah, yes, and it is. My children are not in there and as Mom always says, "A place for everything and everything in its place." For me, my big downfall is other people. *They* mess up my perfectly anal retentive systems. That's not all of it, though. I realized through reading Morgenstern's books, that I'd taken on the task of chief cleaner and bottle washer for years, *never* waking my children to retrieve a pair of shoes from the living room.

The aforementioned Lemmejust Monster became best friends with Critical Dragon and moved in to my life. "Lemmejust mop the kitchen floor before I start dinner." Having done that, "Lemme just empty the dishwasher, *then…*" I'd end up completing twenty-five huge tasks before I'd even begun the main task, which was usually no small one.

Do you do this one? You finally decide that you can't stand it one more moment and you set about cleaning out a room in your home. In transit to other rooms, to return items that belong there, you start ripping apart that room and, before you know what's happened, you're overwhelmed and crying yourself to sleep on the floor. We're apparently supposed to stay focused and keep returning to the original room until it's done. I've been working on that.

Spouses, (not mine, thankfully) can contribute to clutter, making it more overwhelming. My car has looked like a moving dumpster at times when the kids got in the back with their snack bars, bagels and bottles of water. They brought journals (a good thing) and pads of paper for spontaneous art (also a good thing) but then they left it all there. (NOT a good thing.)

Morgenstern references "inconvenient storage" as one breakdown in the organizational system. Inconvenient storage for our kids meant that the containers were not hanging from their armpits and they might have to walk inside to the labeled and sorted containers created for the purpose of sanity control.

"More Stuff than Storage Space," from Morgenstern's system, got tested daily as the hoards of papers came home from all three schools with all three children.

My husband does not participate in what Morgenstern calls "Complex Confusing Systems." He reads the mail over the garbage can and recycling bins, and doesn't concern himself with the notes that say, "Tomorrow is blue day. Your child must wear blue or s/he will be publicly humiliated and emotionally scarred for life. Have a nice day." I'm the one that has been the keeper of such important cryptic messages.

Regarding the system's Out of Sight, Out of Mind focus--let's just say that I've mastered the second part of that. I have gone out of my mind at times—or at least felt like it. Organizing can be very boring or intensely fun, but being organized, ahhh, there's nothing like it.

Morgenstern has broken down various issues into the most logical and useful categories. She explains the external realities that destroy the desire to be neat. Good intentions don't really count here. The external realities (which we all know are created by the mastermind, Critical Dragon) contain five typical stumbling blocks that she has clearly defined in her book.

Psychological obstacles refer to the chaos that has a hidden purpose. This category includes the emotional factors that create self-sabotage. Outlined in this section are ten common pitfalls. This is utterly fascinating because two of them jumped out at me so loudly that I could see, hear and recognize the voice of Critical Dragon from across the street. Sentimental Attachment and Need for Perfection sent me on a journey of discovery.

On another tour, when I requested a show of hands of those who had clutter on the physical plane, all of them raised their hands. When asked who enjoys the clutter, they all lowered them. When I inquired who experiences the clutter as stressful, their hands were, again, raised. They may have connected with different stumbling blocks, but each of them was struggling with the bottom line; clutter.

STORY: Sorting Through the Stuff

This reminds me of a client who came to me with marital issues that she viewed merely as style differences. Clutter was the main issue that was presented. This woman no longer worked in the corporate world, yet continued to buy suits on sale and hang them in her closet, tags on, never to be worn. She also purchased several styles of furniture, had them delivered in order to see which looked the best in a space, and then did not get around to returning the other pieces. Their home was described to me as a warehouse. Oddly enough, the clutter did not bother her because, unlike my experience, clutter to her, felt like home.

As a teenager, she was embarrassed by the clutter in her family's home and pleaded with her mother to clear it. This issue was not resolved back then and she vowed not to let herself get out of control in the same way. However, years later, the clutter represented an unusual source of comfort and also, conflict. Through assessment, one of those pitfalls labeled: The Need for Abundance, proved to be the underlying reason for the clutter. Somehow, to have all of those things around represented a sense of abundance, rather than scarcity. Interesting, too, is how the space itself became scarce and was squeezing the life out of their marriage. Hiding behind all the "stuff" became a way to hide the stuff inside as well.

Morgenstern states that, without this initial assessment, even the best organizational plans will be unsuccessful and that self-criticism will follow. (No kidding. Critical Dragon is sitting in your closet with a journal writing insults to attack you with right now.)

Clearing the clutter makes way for enchantment.

A friend shared with me a simple exercise for clearing physical clutter. It is to touch each item in the cluttered area and ask "Do I love this?" and "Does it serve a purpose?" If you have a "no" answer to both questions, you can get rid of the item.

I told the story of my challenge with this to those I mentioned from an earlier tour. I used to have drawers full of pens that were mostly out of ink. True, they would only write every third word, which is never useful, but how could I throw them out when they still had some ink? I felt guilty. Judging from the enormous response from busted Dragons, I knew I was not alone in this challenge. I still need to tell myself to release the pen, if it cannot be refilled, even though it's pretty or displays the phone number of a place I call frequently. In doing so, I clear space in my life. Try it.

Don Aslett,[45] is here to share another method of cleaning up our lives.

JOURNEY GUIDE

Don Aslett

Housecleaner extraordinaire and author of several books, including Is There Life After Housework? A Revolutionary Approach That Will Free You From the Drudgery of Housework.

Aslett's philosophy on house cleaning is captured in the following statement:

You are entitled to a life of love, fulfillment and accomplishment, but these rewards are almost impossible to obtain when you spend your life thrashing and wallowing in a muddle of housework. Time-the time to love, to be, to grow-is the most precious commodity on earth. No one's time should be wasted cleaning needlessly or inefficiently.

The simple and effective system that Aslett has devised, deals with all kinds of potential clutter. It's a four-step process that categorizes the clutter into containers marked SPROUT, DOUBT, REROUTE and OUT.

The SPROUT file is a place for items to be kept that will be used in the future. Whether one is working toward a doctoral degree or remodeling a kitchen, ideas that will contribute to that project become sprouts that grow into something greater. Aslett states that all of his books have been written from notes shoved into a SPROUT file.

In my opinion, the DOUBT bin, is probably the toughest challenge. That contains the magazines, the mail, the professional conference notes, and all of the items that need attention, but cannot be completed in the moment. Aslett suggests having a container that is large enough to hold about a week's worth of DOUBT material, but not so much that it becomes impossible to transport. He recommends a briefcase, rather than a shopping bag, to hold the contents. He also proposes that people carry it with them to empty during pockets of unexpected time that might otherwise be wasted. For example, the wait in most doctors' or dentists' offices is usually between twenty minutes and two days. That's usually enough time to, at least, begin the process of sorting and purging. Mail, articles, etc. can be thrown out, marked for rerouting or placed in the SPROUT folder.

With regard to magazines, Aslett believes that one should only read through them once. Since seventy-percent of the content in most magazines is advertising, he also suggests that people earmark the pages of those articles or recipes that they think they might like to save. Then they can tear out those pages and recycle the rest. Instead of carting around a whole magazine that gets flipped through repeatedly, thus wasting valuable time, and creating clutter and stress, the ten to twenty pages can be read and further filed. This man is a green-minded genius.

The magazines, ideas that relate to other people's issues, and outgrown clothes, can be REROUTED. So too, can the twenty-six recipes for Thousand Island dressing that have been saved because a friend requested one from you three years ago.

The OUT system is the fourth step. There are items, whether clothing or email, that have been ripped or read, that will never be used again, creating clutter on all planes. Aslett says to throw them out or delete them.

Beyond this system, Aslett's books are full of excellent cleaning suggestions, recipes for removing stains and ways to improve cleaning efficiency.

Feng Shui, the Chinese art of placement, is becoming a household word. Terah Kathryn Collins,[46] is a special one of several Feng Shui specialists.

 **JOURNEY GUIDE**

Terah Kathryn Collins

Registered Polarity practitioner, teacher, and co-founder of the Polarity Therapy Center of Northern Virginia. She left her holistic health care practice and began her life's work as a Feng Shui consultant.

Collins explains:

I was captivated by the notion that holistic health principles apply as powerfully to environments as they do to people. With this in mind, I felt that my new purpose would involve healing and my love for the environment. I filled notebooks with correlations, musings, and notes on my observations of the environmental body.

(This sounds like she may have done some powerful journaling and had a SPROUT file!)

Feng Shui addresses the issues of balance, with regard to the five basic elements of wood, fire, earth, metal and water, direction of the flow of energy, Yin (feminine) and Yang (masculine) energies and filling in vacant spaces that can deplete chi, or life force. The Bagua map is also an essential component, which divides the dwelling space into nine specific areas.

Collins reinforces the notion that people need to surround themselves with things and people that they love in order to achieve balance and harmony.

There is an ancient Chinese saying:

> Being born with good looks is
> not as important as being born
> with a good destiny;
>
> Being born with a good destiny
> is not as important as
> having a kind heart;
>
> Having a kind heart is not as
> important as having a
> positive state of Ch'i.

Lauri Ward,[47] helps us reduce clutter in our physical living spaces.

JOURNEY GUIDE

Lauri Ward

Design consultant who believes in following the basic principles, while inducing a sense of well-being, reducing clutter, and raising awareness of the emotional ties connected to décor and furniture arrangement.

Ward advises the use of a creative plan for the arrangement of furniture, appliances and accessories that already exist in the home or office. She also mentions the importance of observing patterns of decorating that have emotional roots in the family of origin. Ward states that a particular item or placement of an item may be chosen because of its familiarity in a person's childhood home. These choices may even elicit negative feelings, but are unconsciously selected.

For instance, the father may have been emotionally distant, and chose to have his chair in the corner, separate from the area of conversation and family activity. When the child attempts to decorate his or her own home, it may seem right to put the chair in the corner. It may, however, feel wrong. Consideration of whether choices are being made because of past patterns from childhood, or because they are consciously chosen in the present, is important.

Two Master teachers are welcomed now; Henry David Thoreau[48] and Ralph Waldo Emerson[49]. When we're lucky, they continue to walk with us throughout the remainder of our journey.

JOURNEY GUIDES

Henry David Thoreau

Author, naturalist, philosopher, and early environmentalist, Thoreau was best known for Walden, *his written work on living simply, and* Civil Disobedience, *his non-violent resistance to certain laws, in an attempt to improve the government.*

Henry David Thoreau said, "Go confidently in the direction of your dreams! Live the life you've imagined. As you simplify your life, the laws of the universe will be simpler."

Ralph Waldo Emerson

Essayist, poet, philosopher and leader of the Transcendentalist movement, he encouraged the practice of simplicity.

Emerson embodied Transcendental thought with the following statement: "The Transcendentalist adopts the whole connection of spiritual doctrine. He believes in miracle, in the perpetual openness of the human mind to new influx of light and power; he believes in inspiration, and in ecstasy."

Kabat-Zinn offers ideas on simplifying life that address the clutter of activities, as well as belief systems. We all need to consider whether or not we must commit to so many obligations, do as much as we do in each day, have the bombardment of television continuously, use the car as often as we use it, and drive ourselves to make as much money as we believe we need to make. "Giving some thought and attention to the ways in which you might simplify things will probably start you on the road toward making your time your own."

Andrew Weil,[50] assists with clearing mental clutter. Many of you think of this good doctor as "the guy with the big beard."

JOURNEY GUIDE

> # Andrew Weil
>
> *An American born physician and author, Weil is best known for his work in establishing the field of Integrative Medicine.*

With regard to clutter on the mental plane, Weil specifically targets news as a time-consumer and anxiety-inducer. He suggests a regular practice of refraining from listening to the news on the radio, watching it on television, or reading about it in the newspaper. Weil's personal experience with news is that there is more information covered that creates anxiety and anger within him, than that makes him feel good.

This may be true for you, too.

When I ran into a woman about a month after she had taken *The Enchanted Journey* tour, she told me, rather apologetically, that all she had done so far was consider that she had issues with clutter. She said, "All I did was throw away all of the pens that were out of ink." I congratulated her on that and asked her how it felt. "Exhilarating!" she replied. She admitted that it gave her "such a rush" that she was going to tackle her closet next.

Activities:

Reduced Clutter

1. **Select one piece of clutter that exists for you in EACH of the planes: emotional, mental, spiritual and physical, and make a plan toward eliminating it.**
2. **What is your biggest obstacle to a clutter-free environment?** (Even if you have not read any of the books on the subject, yet, you may have a pretty good idea of how Critical Dragon pulls this one off, right in front of you.)
3. **Go through your pens and get rid of the ones that are out of ink or cannot be refilled. Sharpen the broken pencils, next, and throw away the ones that are less than one inch long, even if they still have a point and an eraser.**
4. **Tackle three magazines that are just lying around your space. Use Aslett's method of going through it and then recycle the rest.**
5. **Go into your closet. Select three items that you have not worn in over two years. If the reason is due to a missing button, sew it on and keep it. If not, then let it go to someone else who can wear it now.** (The rule of thumb is usually one year but I know how persuasive Dragons can be!)

Action Plan:

From this moment forward, begin to make conscious choices regarding the clutter in your life. Do not think that you have to begin clearing the clutter created from high school and work forward to now. You can begin with the now.

In the process, you may discover that you have the energy to begin to work back and forth between now and the past messes that have accumulated. Remember to check all of the planes, regularly, including cyberspace, and stay on top of the situation. By the way, Morgenstern has another book titled, *Never Check E-mail in the Morning... and Other Surprising Time Savers.*

Undoubtedly, there will be times that you have greater success with this than during other times.

Elicit the help of your Internal Enchantress and you'll be just fine. You are the proud owner of five keys! You are halfway there.

Chapter Ten: Humor

Figure out what makes you laugh, how you laugh, and how to do it more often. One of the Queens of humor, Erma Bombeck, [51] didn't help us laugh, she made us laugh.

JOURNEY GUIDE

> # Erma Bombeck
>
> *Humorist and writer who began her career as a newspaper columnist, writing about daily life in suburbia. She was the author of several books, including* The Grass is Always Greener Over the Septic Tank, Aunt Erma's Cope Book, *and* If Life is a Bowl of Cherries, What Am I Doing in the Pits?

Bombeck said, "When humor goes, there goes civilization."

In 1969, the editor at the newspaper for which she wrote her column, gave her a daunting task. She was told to "make housewives laugh." Her reply, "I mean no disrespect, sir, but that's like making me photo editor of *Reader's Digest.*"

From 1965, until her death in 1996, Bombeck published more than four thousand syndicated columns and wrote numerous books, in which she used humor to comment on the mundane bits of everyday life that created a bond between her and her readers, and the universe, as a whole.

The actor, Victor Borge is quoted as saying, "Laughter is the shortest distance between two people." I agree. My husband made me laugh within the first few minutes of meeting him and the deal was sealed. Even better than gorgeous eyes or nice, clean fingernails, is the ability to experience humor with another humor being. Have you noticed that people whom you might not find physically attractive at first glance become more so when smiling, laughing and sharing humor? Laughter is contagious and it's good for you. Catch it.

In addition to the psychological effects of humor and laughter, there are a number of physiological effects as well. A good belly laugh exercises the diaphragm, thorax, abdomen, heart and lungs. Initially, when you laugh, your blood pressure and heart rate increase, until they peak. Then there's a decrease, which registers at a healthier, lower level than when your laughter began.

Dr. Lee Berk, [52] believes in the Biblical quote, "A merry heart does good like a medicine."

JOURNEY GUIDE

Lee Berk

Preventive care clinician, medical research scientist, and psychoneuroimmunologist, whose studies revealed that laughter activates the immune system and produces positive emotions.

Berk's studies were pioneering because the research had previously focused on negative stress. His work zeroed in on what he called "mirthful laughter." Berk likened mirthful laughter to a conductor in an orchestra; not playing an instrument but whose influence coordinates all of the separate sections into a harmonious and well-functioning whole. Mirthful laughter lowers blood pressure, reduces stress hormones, increases flexibility in muscles, and boosts immune function by raising levels of infection-fighting T-cells, and the antibodies produced that destroy disease. Laughter also releases endorphins, the body's natural painkillers, and promotes well-being.

So, in essence, it's funny that laughter is one of the few things that feels good, doesn't require birth control, and is actually beneficial for you.

A brilliant man and Master Court Jester, Dr. Joel Goodman,[53] joins us.

JOURNEY GUIDES

Joel Goodman & Matt Weinstein

Goodman is the founder and developer of The Humor Project, which explores the personal, practical and professional applications of humor. Weinstein and Goodman co-authored a book about play.

Years ago, I had the extreme pleasure of attending a Power of Laughter and Play workshop in San Francisco, California. Joel Goodman and Matt Weinstein, co-authors of *Playfair: Everybody's Guide to Noncompetitive Play,* facilitated the workshop. In it, we explored the various types of humor and the reasons we, as individuals, find things funny, offensive or stupid. We also discussed universality in humor.

An example of universality in humor might take place in a movie theatre, with people who don't even speak the same language. All will laugh at visual humor.

Goodman and Weinstein also discussed the idea of inside jokes within racial, ethnic and cultural groups. You may have observed, firsthand, a joke being funny if someone in the same group is the one saying it, whereas if someone outside of the group makes the joke it can be perceived as cruel or even threatening. They made a profound point of teaching that humor is not funny if the laughter is directed at someone, rather than with someone. I came away from that workshop realizing the importance of humor as a tool, not only to heal ourselves, but also, the entire planet.

I vowed to include humor in my practice and had Goodman and Weinstein's blessings to create my own humor project. That was the whole point, after all, to spread the word. Goodman believes that a person's sense of humor affects his or her attitude towards life. He contends that an attitude of childishness is different from a childlike perspective, and that the latter is a mature and developed coping skill.

STORY: Birth of *The Clowning Glory: The Healing Effects of Laughter and Love*

After attending their workshop, I flew home in full flower-child clown regalia. That became my trademark costume; white tunic dress, white tights, white boots, and a crown of flowers on my head, from which flowed multicolored ribbons. I had huge painted eyelashes, red hearts on my cheeks and, of course, a red nose. I created a workshop titled: *The Clowning Glory: the Healing Effects of Laughter and Love*.

A year later, having done the workshop at several facilities in Southern California, I was scheduled to do *The Clowning Glory* at a hospital a few miles from my home. Some of the staff, who had attended a Lunch and Learn elsewhere, invited me.

It was a good thing that my white tunic top had a drawstring because I was very fully nine months pregnant. Thankfully, the rest of my body appeared the same as it had before, but I sported this huge, looked-like-I-had-just-swallowed-a-prize-winning-watermelon belly. The staff members, who had caught my act before, were amused by the humorous addition to my costume. I decided to share with them and the audience that it wasn't a visual prank after a few nurses thumped on my belly and asked what I used for stuffing. "A real baby," I explained.

The audience got so into the humor that on a break, they called a labor and delivery nurse upstairs, filled her in on their joke, and at the end of my program, she came rolling in with a wheelchair saying that there was a pregnant clown needing to be taken up to Labor and Delivery, stat. It was very funny.

Funnier still, was being at that same hospital, two weeks later, and seeing many of those same attendees, when I was in the process of birthing our firstborn. It's important to be able to laugh at yourself at a time like that. (*Very* important.)

Wayne Dyer, whom you've met, suggests that in order to develop a healthy sense of humor and the ability to laugh freely and openly, one must reconnect with the essence of the childlike self that resides within each of us, regardless of our age. He also states that we literally change the chemistry of our bodies when we laugh, by introducing peptides and endorphins into our bloodstream. And for additional cool party chat, Dyer notes that tears produced from laughter have a different chemical makeup than those produced from sadness.

A deeply feeling client of mine created his own emotional category. He put very special bookmarks in his heart to hold dear the people who evoked in him, "laughter through tears." He explained to me how experiencing those emotions simultaneously made him feel whole and connected.

Kabat-Zinn views laughter as a "profoundly healthful state of momentary body-mind integration and harmony."

Patch Adams, [54]delights and heals us on this journey.

JOURNEY GUIDE

Patch Adams

Doctor, clown and activist, who revolutionized the American health care system through the use of laughter, joy and creativity as healing components that every patient deserved to experience.

Adams' vision began as a twelve-year pilot project, during which allopathic and practitioners of alternative medicine worked together in the treatment of 15,000 patients. Healthcare was provided without cost, doctors did not carry malpractice insurance, doctors and patients related to one another from a basis of mutual trust, and time was spent with each patient.

The pilot project gave birth to the Gesundheit Institute, a non-profit foundation. In the mountains of West Virginia, surrounded by forests and waterfalls, a healthcare facility is the embodiment of Adams' dream.

Hey, there's Bernie Siegel.[55] How fortunate we are to brush elbows with him.

JOURNEY GUIDE

Bernie Siegel

Medical practitioner, pediatric and general surgeon, and author, he is an advocate for humanizing medical education and the profession and bringing awareness of the mind/body connection.

Dr. Bernie Siegel, whom we'll get to spend more time with a little later, stops by to share his thoughts about Patch Adams. He says, "Behind his clown-like persona lies a great deal of wisdom, and it often falls to the court jester to speak the truth that those in power need to hear."

One of my very favorite people on this planet, or any other, is Robin Williams.[56]

JOURNEY GUIDE

Robin Williams

Actor and comedian who rose to fame as Mork from Ork, the television character he developed. Mork and Mindy became a spin-off show in which Williams starred, making him a household name. He is known for his quick wit, dialects, and improvisation style. Williams portrayed Patch Adams in the movie by the same name.

STORY: My Cab Ride with Robin Williams

I must tell you about the brief opportunity I had to meet Robin Williams. We shared a short cab ride one summer in New York. Rarely do I lose my words, but he opened the door to the cab after me and asked if I would share it. Of course I said, "Yes!" and then was rendered speechless. I stared at the unnatural bushel of hair on his arms and neck. He noticed and commented, "I'm like a damn monkey, aren't I?" Then he grabbed the hair on his arm and lifted it, making monkey sounds. I laughed really hard and for far too long, before I managed to say something inane like, "I love your body of work." Wow. Ridiculous. (I was in my early twenties but already painfully aware of Critical Dragon's delight.)

We were at my stop and I got out, offering "Robin" some money for the cab that he refused. In my world, he is a healer of astronomical proportions.

John Graham-Pole[57] is just ahead of us.

JOURNEY GUIDE

John Graham-Pole

Children's oncologist, nationally recognized marrow-transplant specialist, and clown. He is also the founder of the Center for the Arts in Healthcare Research and Education and is prominently featured in a video report on its work titled Color My World.

Graham-Pole's unconventional approach to medicine had always included compassion, and more subtly, humor, but after twenty years as an oncologist in the children's cancer unit, he decided he wanted to do more. He became a clown, wearing mismatched socks, using props and setting the stage for humor and healing on the bone marrow unit at Shands Hospital in Florida.

Shands Hospital Arts-in-Medicine program was also developed. Graham-Pole and Mary Lane, an artist and intensive-care nurse, joined forces and assembled a group of artisans to work with the patients in an effort to touch their creative spirit. They believe that even when the physical bodies cannot be mended, the spirit can still be lifted.

The staff includes a writer, a dancer, a painter, a sculptor, two guitarists and a woman who trained as a shaman with Native Americans. The writer encourages journaling. The dancer dances with children who are physically able and invites them to choreograph dances for her to perform, if they are not. In a much-celebrated portion of the program, the painter encourages the patients to paint on 6X6 inch tiles. After 800 of these tiles had been painted and compiled, the permanent Healing Wall in the lobby of the hospital was created.

Norman Cousins [58] is here to inspire us.

JOURNEY GUIDE

Norman Cousins

*Author, professor, political journalist and advocate
of world peace, he beat the odds that his doctors
gave him and outlived his illness by several years.
Laughter was one of the main medicines he used.*

In *Anatomy of an Illness*, Cousins describes how he became an active participant in his own healing from a serious collagen disease which affected his connective tissue. He was given a one-in-five hundred chance of survival. One of his doctors stated that he had never seen recovery from this illness.

Critical Dragon is right on board when these, normally intelligent people offer death sentences that can literally crush the will to live.

Cousins was told that the likely cause of his illness was heavy metal poisoning or the aftereffect of a previous streptococcal infection. On a trip to the Soviet Union, he and his wife had both been exposed to hydrocarbons from diesel exhaust; however, his wife did not exhibit any symptoms. After consideration of a number of factors, Cousins realized that he had been in a state of adrenal exhaustion, and so was less able to handle a toxic experience.

Ten years earlier, he had read Dr. Selye's book, *The Stress of Life,* and recalled that tension, experienced in the emotions, such as intense frustration or suppressed rage, could lead to adrenal exhaustion. To begin his healing journey, he considered the notion that he could replace his anxiety with some degree of confidence. That was the first step in his plan to take charge of his treatment that included a reevaluation of his medication, surroundings and attitude.

Under his doctor's supervision, he began to take large doses of Vitamin C and humor. Cousins rented videos, watched humorous television programs, and was read to by his nurses. He discovered that ten minutes of genuine belly laughter had an anesthetic effect that would give him at least two hours of pain-free sleep.

Wanting to quantify his observations, Cousins began to measure the physiologic changes following his episodes of laughter and noted the cumulative effects. In just over a week, he was able to move parts of his body without pain. Over the next several weeks and months he recovered enough to be able to return to work as the editor of the *Saturday Review*. Laughter, Vitamin C, and his will to live, proved to be a powerful combination for Cousins.

Taking a look at ways to invite humor into your life can be a fun and enjoyable project, but with Critical Dragon arms waving in front of you, finding humor in this current world we live in, takes conscious effort. Gloom and negativity can be found around every corner, but guess what? If you're on the lookout, humor and positivity are there for your discovery, too.

The road actually travels back to altered perceptions because sometimes humor can be found in the mundane and reframed. For example, in the crimes section of a small-town newspaper a blurb read, "All of the commodes at the police station have been stolen. The police have no leads and nothing to go on." That's funny stuff!

Let me tell you about humor boards and books and how to make them. A humor board can display themed humor, "inside joke" humor, or whatever you'd like it to display. Cards, sayings on T-shirts, comic strips, etc. can be exhibited on tri-fold science boards or a cork bulletin board and posted at home, in a dorm, a classroom, or at the office. You can also include photos or newspaper clippings with captions that you write. Use your imagination and have fun. Children and pets are wonderful sources of humor. A humor book can be a notebook with sheet protectors or a photo album. You can even get fancy and scrapbook the pages.

One tour of nurses wrote to me to say that they had put up a humor board at the nurses' station. They competed with one another to bring in funny stories, cards and cartoons to add to the board. They put up "inside joke" catch phrases that no one else would understand, reminding them of particular incidents which sent them into peals of laughter. In addition, they made a humor book so that when they rotated the board, they could preserve the previous items that had already been displayed. A surgeon at that hospital started a trend of entering the O.R. with a joke, to ease the tension.

STORY: The Humor Book

As part of *The Enchanted Journey Tour*, I share stories from my own personal humor book. A favorite of mine centers around my then, four-year old daughter and nine-month old son. One morning, upon awakening, my son's little sweaty head gave him the appearance of having had his first haircut.

I exclaimed, "Sweetheart! Did elves come in during the night and cut your hair?" My daughter also commented with shock, fearing that she had not been present for his first haircut.

"No," I assured her, "elves must have come in during the night and cut his hair." She knew I was teasing about the elves, as I explained that his hair was just arranged tightly against his head.

Upon arriving at preschool, all the teachers remarked about his hair, as well. After the first stock "elves" response, my daughter was ready to answer the next person who said something. Sure enough, another mother mentioned his hair and my dear daughter chimed in with, "Elvis came in during the night and cut his hair."

That story is a classic in our book.

Also a source of humor and joy are the funny words that kids use to call things while learning to master the language, such as my son's excited pronouncement of "I love mucis." That one grossed a number of people out until I translated quickly that, "He loves *music*--music."

One of my daughters used to think that she had the day off from school in November for Veterinarian's Day.

Our son turned three during my pregnancy with our third child. He'd pat my growing belly and, at eye level, ask directly into the naval mouthpiece, "Are you in there still growing and shining?" It was so sweet that I wanted to remember it always and so thought about starting a sweetness book, but decided I could just add it to the humor book. It evokes an equally healing "Aw" response.

When his sister was born and came home from the hospital, I heard his small voice over the airwaves of the baby monitor. He had crept into her room when she was stirring. He whispered to her, identifying himself with his full name, and then added, "I am your brother and your best friend and I am going to marry you when you grow up, and when you are older, I will paint your toenails." I experienced my client's "laughter through tears," and added that to the book of warm memories.

When my baby girl was four years old, she came down with a nasty virus that had her battling a fever, spewing from every port, and congested for a full week. I took care of her, made special meals for her, as well as healing remedies, and slept by her side. I was overjoyed when she was well and happily bouncing around the house again. She handed me a card that she had made after her recovery, thanking me for taking such good care of her. In it was a five dollar bill she had retrieved from her piggy bank. When I asked what that was for, she said that she sees me pay at the doctor's office and he doesn't even come over to cook or have sleepovers.

That, too, was one for the books.

Comedians such as Jerry Seinfeld, Adam Sandler, Ben Stiller, and Chris Rock, are the newer generation, joining the ranks of the much loved comedians Ann Meara and Jerry Stiller (Ben's parents), Billy Crystal, Whoopi Goldberg, and Dennis Miller. Thankfully, there are many, many more. Sitcoms and comedy shows all help us relax and de-stress.

Jay Leno,[59] who filled the role of the late-night television icon, Johnny Carson, as host of *The Tonight Show*, has made a career of making us laugh.

JOURNEY GUIDE

Jay Leno

Observational humorist who pokes fun at newsworthy issues and everyday life.

In addition to his stand-up opening routines that dealt with topics in the news, Leno filmed a segment for the show called "Jaywalking," in which he asked people on the street basic intelligence or current event questions. He also brought us the Headlines, once a week, in which typos, grammatical errors and double entendres offered opportunities for humor. One that has stayed with me over the years was a supermarket ad for "boneless bananas."

An angel of whimsy, humor, and art, Mary Engelbreit,[60] enchants us.

JOURNEY GUIDE

Mary Engelbreit

*Prolific artist and author
acknowledges life's difficulties and pokes fun at
them in an attempt to lighten our mood.*

Engelbreit has an enchanted key in the humor department, as well as in the arts. Her whimsical images of children and pets on cards, posters, clothing, and all sorts of life's accessories, wax philosophical and humorous, as they order us to "Snap out of it," or demand that we "Put the fun back in dysfunctional."

STORY: Humor's a Riot

Laughter is universal, but humor can be such a personal thing. An ironic situation occurred on one of my tours. The group was discussing humor and what's funny, as perceived by each individual, when a fight ensued!

A man stated that Don Rickles was his favorite comedian. Rickles is a comedian who says that he loves all people but targets various racial and ethnic groups in his humor.

A woman called out that Joan Rivers was her favorite. Rivers is known for her self-deprecating humor.

The man went on to say that "Joan Rivers isn't funny because she's just someone with low self-esteem and that isn't funny; it's pathetic."

The woman stood up and lashed out verbally to the man, saying, "Don Rickles isn't funny because he just points to people, mimics them, and stereotypes them based on race, religion or ethnicity. If you think that that's funny, then there's something wrong with you."

Within moments, people were taking sides and screaming at one another about what is funny.

Hmmmm.

I started to literally tap dance to get their attention and then shared with them what I had just observed: People were on the verge of becoming violent with one another in defense of what they think is funny.

Funny, isn't it?

Everyone calmed down and I was relieved that I didn't have to change into my clown riot gear. The outburst did lead to a passionate discussion about humor.

Another interesting phenomenon addresses the judgments we harbor about the way people laugh. Take a moment to consider how you laugh. What does it actually sound like? Are you a quiet chuckler, a loud cackler, does your laugh span several octaves, are you a snorter or don't you ever find anything funny enough for you to know what your laughter sounds like?

I've always been a rather genteel spirit, but sometimes when I'd laugh it would come from deep within my belly and burst forth in an unrestricted, throaty explosion. I experienced some raised eyebrows and so, just after my college days, I consciously changed my laugh. It's still genuine and spontaneous but somehow less like a longshoreman.

Do you notice your own judgments about laughter? Some people are perceived as insincere and phony by the way they laugh. Others leave the imagined and silently agreed upon "normal" range and slip into "now you are scaring me" laughter. Others, still, are just creepy. So, make no mistake, we all have rules about what's acceptable with regard to laughter, both in pitch, duration, and facial expressions.

I've become keenly aware of laughter and other people's reactions to it. Remember how, when you were a kid, it was so much fun to hold your arms out, spin in circles until you were deliriously dizzy and fall down on the ground laughing? How many people consistently tried to stop you from doing that? Unless your parents grew up practicing Sufi dancing, they were probably not too comfortable with it.

Adults stop children from laughing all of the time. The famous punitive parental says something like, "Okay. That's enough." What does that mean? Have they had enough of energy that appears out of control? Did their stopwatch laugh meter sound an alarm? It was "okay," but now it has crossed the line into "enough?" How do they know? Is it one of those things you get when you become a parent, like eyes in the back of your head?

I remember being told all of the time, when I was out-of-control laughing, "That's enough." (It never really was!) In all fairness to my family, they suffered the ill effects of the time I was laughing hysterically at dinner, which was definitely not allowed when Daddy wanted to watch the news after a long, hard day at work. I was drinking hot chocolate, with those mini-marshmallows in it, and just couldn't help myself. Everyone was stunned and maybe a little disgusted, when I aspirated one of those mini-marshmallows. It traveled its course before it flew out of my nose. (Sorry, but it still makes me laugh.) I behaved for a few years until I did it again. This time it was with a strand of spaghetti with marinara sauce. I'm lucky that I'm still not serving time in my room.

What I noticed as a residual effect of these experiences is that I, myself, became a wee bit tense when my children start laughing with food in their mouths. Laughter in the car, on a playground, or in the backyard was different. But when it came to food, my world was shaded by my past.

We've actually had many meals in which the entire family was left wearing the aftermath of a Vaudevillian spit take from one of the kids. Trust me; it's much funnier when the marshmallow is coming out of your own nose than that of your child's.

I clearly became the dud of our household at the dinner table. I had always envisioned lively discussions about Shakespeare's use of humor or how the work of Anton Chekov, although perceived as being depressing, is actually quite funny.

More often than not during meals, we've had explicit reenactments of all of the Austin Powers movies; accents included. "Oh, behave!" My husband, when he was no longer able to fulfill his parental duty and keep everyone in line, would split his sides laughing. The dirty job of crowd control fell to me. Critical Dragon whispered of the impending doom inherent in laughing while eating peas but my Internal Enchantress restored balance.

Over the years I've had several opportunities to see a range of perspectives on humor in action. Once, when the three kids were young and in the back seat of the car, one of them had some gastrointestinal outbursts. They all fell into fits of laughter. My husband, who was driving, joined them. I've never found bathroom humor to be funny but I know a memory was made that day that will be enjoyed forever.

Everything was funny to them after that, and I made an entry in the humor book when we returned home. Our son, who had been laughing in the way that continues long after he has run out of breath, heaved a sigh as he calmed down, and said, "Aaah. I'm all laughed out." Then he pondered that thoughtfully and added, "But if anything else funny happens, I can still laugh." I found *that* to be very funny and everyone looked at me like I was crazy. It didn't diminish my joy. It did, however, make the point about how one person's funny bone may be located in a different place than in another.

A student-teacher from an enchanted tour several years ago, reported feeling good about his use of humor on his first day of teaching. He had realized during the tour that he valued his sense of humor, as did others, but that he had kept it separate from his academic life. He could barely contain his joy when he said that his students told him he was "cool" because he used humor in his teaching and in his control of the classroom.

Humor is a powerful form of healing medicine. The longevity of George Burns, Lucille Ball, Milton Berle, Red Skelton, Erma Bombeck and Bob Hope, may attest to that. Their lives were certainly not without challenges or pain. Humor, however, fully exercised, becomes a conscious choice that can alter your perspective on life.

Activities:

Humor

1. **What do you find funny and why?**
2. **Think back to a time when someone laughed at you. Recall how isolating it felt. Have compassion for the person who laughed at you and for yourself, then. Vow never to laugh at others.**
3. **What did you learn about humor from your family of origin?**
4. **List as many ways possible, that you can add humor into your life, (in spite of the noise Critical Dragon makes.)**
5. **Create a humor book and/or humor board.**
6. **Laugh out loud as you collect Key #6.**

Action Plan:

Begin to incorporate humor into your daily life. Create a library of funny videos, listen to comedy on radio, record sitcoms that make you laugh. Read humorous books, go to comedy clubs, open discussions about humor (keeping perspective in mind!) and consider whether or not your brand of humor needs tweaking. Reflect on whether or not you use humor to mask other emotions. You're the proud owner of key #6. Enjoy humor and use it in good health.

Chapter Eleven: Movement

<u>**Key #7**</u>

Recharge your battery. Shake your groove thing. Enhance productivity, relieve stress from your body and help your organs function at their best.

Please put everything down and stretch. Now I realize that may be awkward for you if you're rereading this in a car, on a train, in the loo, or in class, but it may also provide you with your first humor book entry. Do the Hokey Pokey, turn yourself around, whatever it takes to move you. Ah.

Benefits

There are many benefits to exercise and just as many ways to achieve them. Skip with me through the gate and I'll tell you more.

Shealy hails adequate physical exercise as one of the greatest stress reducers known. He suggests that an optimal exercise plan includes cardiovascular exercise, as well as limbering or stretching exercises, four to six days a week. He also believes that enough physical exercise increases your tolerance for social, emotional and even chemical stress.

Louise Hay[61] is a prominent Queen of the New Thought movement. She's here to share her wisdom about exercise as well.

JOURNEY GUIDE

Louise Hay
Author of self-help books, such as You Can Heal Your Life, *that focus on the mind-body connection and healing physical ailments through repair of emotional blocks. A cancer survivor, herself, Hay is also the founder of The Hay House; a publishing house dedicated to promoting books and authors of holistic health. Her charitable organization is called the Hay Foundation.*

Hay states that movement strengthens our bones and keeps our bodies youthful. She believes in variety when it comes to choosing forms of exercise, such as weight-bearing workouts, swimming, sports, dancing or martial arts.

What's important is selecting a form of exercise that you'll continue to do regularly. Some people choose how they'd like to stay fit, seasonally, by swimming in summer and skiing in winter, while others just switch periodically, to keep it interesting.

Rice, whom we met at the Altered Perceptions gate, gives us a list from his book, *Stress and Health: Principles and Practice for Coping and Wellness,* of the benefits of exercise, beyond those mentioned above. They include such things as increased respiratory capacity, muscle tone, strength, energy, metabolism, circulation and a host of other perks for the physical body.

Rice also mentions the mental benefits of exercise, such as feelings of self-control, confidence, alertness, improved self-esteem with regard to body image and the reduction of stress. He sites runner's euphoria as a mental benefit of exercise that many athletes experience. Those elated or transcendent feelings are so powerful, that an effort to recreate those feelings often becomes the motivation for continued exercise.

Yoga

Today, people practice yoga for relaxation, moving meditation, enhanced muscle tone and flexibility, and for improved health.

Yoga is a Sanskrit word meaning, "union." The practice of yoga unifies the mind/body, and extends to the union or connection between an individual and the entire universe.

The roots of yogic practice are in India. Yoga is a series of *Asanas,* or physical postures, which are accompanied by breathing techniques, called *Pranayamas.* The first systematic record of the use of yoga, as a way of life, is included in the *Yoga Sutras.* This writing contains a philosophy that embodies strict ethical and moral conduct codes in an eightfold path that begins with ethical teachings, and progresses through control over body postures, breath and withdrawal of the senses. The purpose of achieving mastery over the body is to also gain mastery over the mind.

Elliott Dacher[62] joins us.

JOURNEY GUIDE

Elliott Dacher
An internal medicine doctor who believes in integral health and healing. Dacher is the author of Integral Health: The Path to Human Flourishing Whole Healing and Intentional Healing. *His view is that we not only have the power within ourselves to simply survive but, also, to flourish.*

Dacher contends that stress, knowing it wasn't called that in ancient times, is not a condition present only in modern times. He references Asian culture three thousand years ago, during which time men and women discovered that there was stress inherent in daily living conditions and also, that there was a need to develop methods for relieving this pain and suffering.

Introspection became a meditative means of relief for many. For others, yoga, in combination with proper thinking, attitudes and life-style was the pathway to relieve pain and suffering.

Way back then, the ancient yogis realized that stress was a result of an internal perception about an external circumstance. They knew that people's attitudes, perceptions and lifestyle choices were central to determining their responses to events outside of themselves and whether or not they would suffer from disease.

Weil specifically recommends yoga for people who have been diagnosed with hypothyroidism. Hypothyroidism is classified by under-active thyroid conditions. The shoulder stand pose stimulates the thyroid and increases blood flow to the area. Weil suggests that this pose is even more effective if used in combination with visualization.

Kabat-Zinn touts the benefits of yoga as a full-body conditioner and toner that's gentle and can be practiced at various levels of conditioning. It can be done daily, if desired, and while sitting, standing, or lying on the floor, as well as on a chair, bed, or even in a wheelchair.

Although it's a form of meditation, another benefit is its energizing effect. A posture, some movement and breath are all that's required to begin the practice of yoga. Kabat-Zinn states "every time you intentionally assume a different posture, you are literally changing your physical orientation and therefore your inner perspective as well." He also proposes that people can experience feelings of happiness and relaxation just by using the muscles it takes to mimic a smile.

Check it out right now. Smile. See if you feel happier. Notice if this smiling thing is foreign to you. If you've never experienced laughing, begin with smiling. Work your way up to belly laughing.

Carlson was also a big supporter of the practice of yoga for its physical and emotional benefits. He's been quoted as saying:

On the physical side, yoga strengthens the muscles and the spine, creating flexibility and ease of motion. On the emotional side, yoga is a tremendous stress reducer. It balances the body-mind-spirit-connection, giving you a feeling of ease and peace.

It's time for a break.

 Dragon Alert! "Don't take breaks!"

Ignore that.
- Sit in a relaxed posture, either in a chair or cross-legged on the floor.
- Take a deep and cleansing breath, in through the nose, and exhale, out through the mouth. Repeat.
- Assume a prayer posture, with the palms of the hands pressed together at the fourth chakra, in the center of the chest, aligned with the heart. This posture is also called, "Namaste," which is a Sanskrit word, loosely translated to mean, "The Higher-Self/Divine Source in me recognizes and honors the Higher-Self/Divine Source in you."
- Hold this posture for a few moments, just tracking your breath as it moves in and out of your body. Make no attempt to alter it. Just observe it.
- Notice tension in your body and breathe into it to release it.

Yoga practice includes various postures whose names reflect the movement itself, such as sun salutation, in which the arms are lifted upward and widened, as if embracing the sun. The gaze is upward and comes down as the arms are lowered. Try it.

Down dog resembles a second grader doing a push up, with weight distributed on all fours, legs and arms extended, but with the rear end up in the air.

Then there's lion pose. Send an engraved invitation for Critical Dragon to show up for this one. It involves releasing your mouth like a lion yawning and sticking your tongue out and down as far as possible, while opening your eyes wide, without popping them out of their sockets. Yeah, Critical Dragon loves this one because there's no doing it half way. Go ahead. Try it right now. And I *do* remember that you may be continuing your journey at your ob/gyn's office or while waiting for the NASDAQ report. Once you get past Critical Dragon's assurance that you look like an idiot, it feels rather good, doesn't it?

Another stop on our trip through movement offers another form of yoga designed by Darrin Zeer[63].

JOURNEY GUIDE

Darrin Zeer
Relaxation expert and author of Office Yoga, Simple Stretches for Busy People.

Office Yoga

Office yoga is a twenty-first century version of the yoga mentioned earlier. It also includes breathing techniques and body postures, however, they're designed for people who will be performing them at their computers and/or desks. The purpose is to relieve stress.

Specific exercises target areas of stress, such as the tension lodged in your neck and shoulders. With computers at the center of work and home, eyestrain and mental fatigue are commonly experienced problems as well. Fingers are also a focus because they're held in rigid positions on the keyboard and mouse all day. They need release and movement that maintain their flexibility. This kind of yoga is user-friendly because any attire can be worn, the techniques are quick and the effects are long lasting.

Neck and shoulder rolls, performed right in your chair, release tight muscles. Wherever you are right now, roll your neck around like we did earlier. Another tense muscle reliever for neck and shoulders uses the natural weight of your hands laced on the back of your head. Look down and gently press your hands downward. Leaving your hands laced on the back of your head, create resistance as you press upward with your head. This releases and relaxes a different set of muscles.

To loosen up stiff back muscles, use an office chair as a prop, and slowly twist to grasp the back of your chair with both hands. With slow and steady motion, stretch your back muscles. Then twist in the opposite direction.

In another chair exercise, bend over from the waist and allow your head to rest gently on your knees. Let your arms fall down, on either side, to the floor. Please be sure to have pushed your chair far enough away from your desk so that you don't bang your head. If you continually forget to do this, you may wish to keep some butterfly bandages in your drawer. Don't suddenly drop over in your seat during group presentations, as it can result in calls to the paramedics from your colleagues. (Ask me how I know.)

To relieve eye strain, picture a big clock in front of you. Move your eyes to look up at the top position or 12 o'clock. Put the twelve up as high as you can comfortably look, while still offering your eyeballs a bit of a stretch. Then move your eyes completely around the clock, pausing at each number. When you've arrived at the starting point again, reverse the process and look to 11 o'clock, 10 o'clock, and so on, until you have arrived back at the beginning again. You may wish to do this exercise every hour or so that you're on the computer, to refresh yourself.

Tai Chi

The American Heart Association determined that the practice of tai chi lowers blood pressure in senior citizens nearly as much as walking briskly.

Weil also supports this form of exercise because, in addition to its effects on blood pressure, it also develops flexibility and balance, and aids in stress reduction and relaxation.

Dance

Gabrielle Roth[64] dances her way onto our path.

JOURNEY GUIDE

Gabrielle Roth

A "trance dancer" who combines contemporary music, theatre, and poetry with shamanic rhythms and healing power.

Roth refers to bodies as "cradles of the soul." Isn't that beautiful? Her formula for healing includes "sweating your prayers." She wrote a book titled *Sweat Your Prayers*, which combines her background in theatre, various forms of dance, movement therapy, and ritual and shamanic practice, in order to teach others to move beyond the personality of the ego and release emotions as a path toward ecstasy.

In *Roth's 5 Rhythms*, five universal rhythms are defined, each with its own archetype. They are as follows: flowing, staccato, chaos, lyrical and stillness. Roth observes a correlation between the progression of rhythms in nature and life's events. Whether referencing lovemaking or childbirth, these rhythms are present. She suggests that we learn to identify our own personal rhythms, as well as practice all of them, in order to evolve with a sense of wholeness. Roth also believes that pain can be detoxed through the sweat and prayers that are danced. Roth's son, Jonathan Horan, often teaches with her.

This Enchantress took one of Jonathan's classes and it was a transcendent experience, dancing in a very crowded space, at times, with our eyes closed. Dragons oozed out through the pores.

During previous tours I had included a three-minute selection of contemporary music, during which participants were invited to simply move various parts of their bodies to the rhythms. Even though I did the movements with them and didn't use the "D" word, (dance), the suggestion to move the body created stress for many people.

It's been interesting to observe the cultural and racial differences among Dragons. The loudest Critical Dragons jeering from the sides of the dance floor, that I've experienced, have been from Caucasian participants. There was a great deal of self-conscious behavior.

One time, during a tour with a predominantly African-American audience, I observed only one or two Dragons present during the movement portion. For those two people, however, the overwhelming feelings of inadequacy and shame were painful. The three of us discussed it, afterward, and they expressed concerns about isolation and alienation from a culture that not only encourages movement, but also celebrates it.

Participants from Latin cultures have also been exuberant. They, too, were not afraid to move their bodies, whereas five Asian participants, there, together in the group, were more reserved. They joked about wanting to go into the restroom until that part of the journey was over.

Those who did take part in the movement period assessed their stress levels following the three-minute exercise. They unanimously reported feeling more relaxed, joyful and lighter. All of this was accomplished in under five minutes.

Walking Meditation

Walk with me.

Kabat-Zinn discovered that walking meditations have a potent effect on people suffering from anxiety-related conditions.

While Cameron regards Morning Pages and Artist's Dates as vital components in the process of healing and self-discovery, she also purports that walking, as a form of meditation, releases the creative spirit.

Once again, you see how all of these keys you're acquiring are interrelated and useful.

A previous tour participant shared with me that she knew she needed to exercise and meditate but found those activities to be boring. She'd abandoned her plans to lose weight and find time to be introspective until she learned about walking meditations. Six months later, she contacted me to say that on the evening of her tour, she tried it and it was enjoyable. She had continued this practice, intermittently, for the next three weeks, and alternated between connection to nature through sensory awareness of the trees, flowers, wind on her face, etc., and contemplation of an issue. She didn't want to tell anyone about it because then people would be "watching" to be sure she stayed with her routine. People did, however, notice the results and told her that she appeared to be more toned and relaxed. It became part of her daily routine and on days when it rains or she is unable to walk, she journals, returning to the walking meditations as soon as she can.

This freedom aids the expression of the mind, spirit and emotions, while also tuning the physical instrument. Cameron suggests that, in addition to walking, you also practice walking "prayerfully." This gives you the opportunity to express feelings of gratitude. Along with daily twenty-minute walks, at least once a week, an hour-long walk is required, and then, once or more a week, an intentional prayerful walk is suggested. Cameron invites you to make a list of everything that you're grateful for, and vocalize it while you walk.

Meister Eckhart, the fourteenth century mystic, noted that if "thank you" is the only prayer we say in our whole lives that would be sufficient. Holding that thought, you could visualize everything you're thankful for, as you step in rhythm to "thank you," "thank you," "thank you." Walking while speaking your prayers is only slightly more advanced than walking while chewing gum. Practice makes you practiced; not perfect, so feel free to give it a try.

Bodywork

There are various forms of bodywork, performed by other people on your body, which are considered beneficial. Some of these techniques include Rolfing, Heller Work or Trager, massage, foot reflexology, acupuncture, chiropractic, Alexander Method, Bioenergetics, Feldenkrais, Touch for Health and Reiki.

Physical therapists have two sayings for people who desire to take better care of their bodies. The first is, "If it is physical, it's therapy," meaning that it doesn't matter what form of physical exercise you're engaged in, but that you're involved in some form of physical activity. The second is, "If you don't use it, you lose it." That refers to the decline in muscle mass and flexibility that occurs if the muscles atrophy from lack of use.

(The same can be said about perspective.)

Years ago, treatment for heart patients following a heart attack, was bed rest. Current treatment involves exercise and walking within a few days following the attack. Even a heart whose arteries have been hardened by arteriosclerosis becomes stronger as it responds to the challenge of regular, graduated exercise.

Critical Dragon is the one whining about how exercise isn't fun and that it's too expensive to buy the right clothes, you get too sweaty, and a litany of other excuses.

With Critical Dragon's willing assistance, you may have discovered that activities which, for years, brought you great joy and physical toning now are a drag. (Note to self: when something is a "drag," or a situation "drags on," you can be pretty sure that the "Dragon" is in charge of it. It's just another way of showing up.)

STORY: Moved to Tears

I'd signed up for professional level dance classes to get back in shape, after my final chapter of childbirth. I'd been a professional dancer for years, and loved it. I knew I'd be a little rusty but I wasn't prepared for what I experienced. Critical Dragon reached a new depth of evil. Childbirth for the third time resulted in a slight loss of muscle tone and flexibility but Critical Dragon called me an "old bag," in that mirrored room and compared me to the twenty-year olds who danced alongside of me.

Those groans I heard were coming from me during the "twelve o'clock kicks." Those are what the Radio City Music Hall Rockettes are famous for; in a line, arms out to the sides, around the shoulders of other dancers, and kicking up toward the number twelve on an imaginary clock. I'll tell you how I know. Those same Radio City Music Hall Rockettes had rejected me, after several callbacks, twenty years earlier because my left leg could only muster maybe 11:15 on the clock.

What was I thinking taking a professional level class again? I was in my forties, dancing with twenty-year olds who were in mortal danger of being hit by my flapping thighs. My body betrayed me. I had carried people around inside of it and now it wasn't going to do what I needed it to do, when I needed it to do it. Dancing wasn't fun anymore. You know who came up with that loaded thought. Critical Dragon wagged her tutu'd derriere in my face while I cried. A change of perspective was in order.

My Internal Enchantress, whom I didn't really know at the time, reminded me that I love to dance, that, especially because my livelihood no longer was dependent upon it, I could still dance whenever the spirit moved me.

I vowed to dance at home and signed up for a martial arts class. My then, seven-year old daughter wanted to join me. That was perfect because it provided an opportunity to get into butt-kicking shape, while also bonding, on yet another level, with my daughter. What was amazing about choosing something with which I had no experience was that, instead of Critical Dragon really being able to step up to the plate to torture me about that, I felt free to make mistakes because there were no expectations about being good at it.

What a blast! My two-piece karate *ghi* was black and fabulously slimming, while the white belt provided a nice fashion contrast and accentuated my thinning waist. I sculpted rock-hard muscles. My *sensei* taught me to develop a *kiai*. It's a yell that translates, literally, into concentrated spirit. When done correctly, it can stun small animals, and, as a perk, also large Critical Dragons. Even when I got knocked out during my first *shiai* (competition) while sparring with a female fire fighter, I didn't quit. With the last ounce of sense that I had, I crawled out of the ring, but stayed to win a first place trophy in *kata*, (the solo choreographed patterns of movement.) Guess why? Yes, because of my dance background.

Today, I'm in dance classes again. I hip-hop and Afro-Brazilian dance my way to vibrant health. I also do yoga, Pilates, recumbent bike and weight-bearing exercise to round out each week.

Walt Whitman said in 1856, in his *Song of the Open Road,* "Loos'd of limits and imaginary bounds, I am larger, better than I thought."

Activities:
Movement
1. **Do this as a journal exercise. What is your favorite form of movement to engage in and why?**

2. **Write about all the ways that Critical Dragon keeps you from engaging in movement regularly.**
3. **What thoughts and feelings come up for you when you align yourself with Critical Dragon and feel guilty, apathetic, unmotivated, bored, etc. for not adding movement into your life?**
4. **What movement would you be willing to add into your routine?**
5. **Using Gabrielle Roth's rhythms of flowing, staccato, chaos, lyrical and stillness as starting places, what is your predominant rhythm in the world?**
6. **Add Key #7 to your keychain.**

Action Plan:

Begin to incorporate some form of movement into your life each day. You can start with five minutes of movement, but get started today. Work up to twenty or thirty minutes a day. Even if, upon awakening, you twirl around in circles in one direction and then spin around in the other direction to unwind, that's movement. Walk the dog, sweat your prayers, park in the farthest spots, use the stairs instead of elevators, jump an imaginary jump rope (you never miss that way) and, as the popular children's musician suggests, "shake your sillies out and wiggle your waggles away." Your endorphin release will have you coming back for more. Keep it moving and shake it, so you don't break it.

Chapter Twelve: Art

Key #8

Play with shapes, colors, textures, and images to create a journal without words.

If you think your Critical Dragon had you in a body lock during the movement portion, just try making some art! Whether or not you had this art teacher, everyone remembers as if they had, the teacher who became very tense around the corners of her mouth unless you drew the wide, brown tree trunk, round circles of green leaves at the top and perfectly symmetrical red apples nestled in those leaves. The sky was blue the clouds were white, the sun, yellow. Drawing birds and the occasional flower was acceptable. Black crayons were not. They were "too messy" but could be requested by a child who had to color a black cat or during Halloween, but otherwise, were removed from the box lest children scare their classmates with dark renderings of their innermost dysfunctions.

STORY: My Art Teacher, Sleeping Beauty

I remember my first grade art teacher, Miss Smith. I thought she was Sleeping Beauty. She had straight, blonde hair and greenish-blue eyes. She had pale skin, too, that I decided, back then, was from eating too much paste.

One of the reasons I liked her was that she understood I was a serious artist. I wasn't there to chew the crayon paper off in a ring or take a bite out of the purple crayons to see if they were grape flavored. No. I wanted to make pretty pictures. I didn't want to have to "fill the page, fill the page," as I had already been previously instructed to do.

To me, drawing myself at six years of age on the bottom corner of the picture, as tiny girl with blonde, curly hair and arms coming out of my face, didn't mean that I had no neck and low self-esteem. So I had left my neck out of the drawing. Big deal. So I made myself small, in the corner of the page. I didn't personally care for the kids who drew themselves on the entire sheet, without room for anyone or anything else. No one ever actually asked me if I suffered from low self-esteem. They just kept telling me to make myself bigger, bigger. As we now know, bigger is not always better. I was wise beyond my years. (I still rebel, in my own little good-girl way, by putting objects off center and not filling the page.)

I loved that clean sheet of Manila paper we were given. I hated the feel of it on the palm of my hand. Ugh. It still sends shivers down my spine. It reminded me of those flat, Velda Farms wooden spoons that came with the small, ice cream cups. (The reason I didn't keep up with playing the clarinet, later in school, was because licking the reed was too much like licking those little, wooden spoons.)

But I digress. That sheet of Manila paper in art class came only one to a customer. If you made a mistake, you had to turn the paper over. If you made another mistake, that was too bad. I hated that part. (I give my clients and children lots of paper to use, and then keep planting trees to make up for it.)

Anyway, thank goodness I didn't let the feel of the paper or the restrictions keep me from making art. It's pure joy.

All of this is a build-up to the importance of surrounding yourself with materials that you love and having a blank canvas, of some sort, on which to create. It can be a clear computer screen with web page design possibilities, a pencil on a clean sheet of paper drawing countless lines, a canvas waiting to be splashed with acrylic paint, or heavy watercolor paper on which to float a river of colors. An empty mat on which to make beaded jewelry holds the same enchantment. I love them all.

Not everyone does. Art can be very intimidating. My husband's Critical Dragon keeps the supplies locked in a dungeon somewhere. It's the same place in which my mother-in-law's Critical Dragon kept hers. She never made art because she was taught not to make messes. In addition, she believes that nothing short of heroic courage is required to commit an idea to the page. She's also terrified to make a mistake. Is it any wonder that my husband never attempted art until I forced him? Of course I mean, *encouraged.*

My husband has been present at several of these tours where, if he had refused to draw, might have been strung up in brightly colored ribbons and dragged through town by reformed Critical Dragons. On those occasions, he has drawn. I have framed his work and display it proudly.

Surprisingly, his dear grandmother, at the age of ninety-five, began painting when she moved into a nursing facility, as a form of expression in her final months on this earth. She, who had never painted, showed a true gift. I'd bet that my mother-in-law, too, possesses a hidden talent. I'll keep nudging her to express it before she's ninety-five.

Creating the space in which to create, no matter how small, can be inspiring. A brand new box of sharpened 64 Crayola crayons has always thrilled me. In my art room, I have a visual explosion of color on the turntable of colored markers and pencils. I also have decorative scissors, watercolor paints, handmade paper the kids and I have made, and some of their raw, primitive, from-the-soul art. Even when I don't have time to sit down at the art table, it's like eye candy that gets the creative juices flowing.

Thacher Hurd and John Cassidy[65] arrive with an invitation to play.

JOURNEY GUIDE

Hurd & Cassidy

Artists and authors of the fun and informative playbook, Watercolor for the Artistically Undiscovered, *who refer to art as personal expression.*

They believe that art is born from each individual's talent and no one else can reproduce someone else's talent. They say, "The only mistake you can make is to criticize yourself, get in your own way—or to start straining and stop having fun." In his "Ironclad Rule of Spirited Watercolors," Hurd supports the artist within by reminding us that we are better than we think we are.

Tell the truth. How many times have you walked through a gallery or museum and whispered to yourself or someone else, "I could do that!" You could. My husband could. Chances are that you just didn't. They did.

One time I saw, in a well-known gallery, a black wall created in front of which was a white ceramic toothbrush holder, holding a white toothbrush. People were standing before it, eyes squinted, oohing and aahing as they contemplated the art. I had to throw my coat over my husband's head to muffle his outbursts about this art that he thought was ridiculous and insulting. I felt the same way but was too busy ushering him out the door so our membership would not be revoked that early in the season.

You've heard the expression, "Beauty is in the eye of the beholder." Maybe those eyes were just closed. Maybe mine are. I decided I would just go back another day and figure out what the artist was trying to say to me. I wonder, cynically, if some artists are not saying anything at all. Maybe they're just hanging around, bemused by the few who may stand there, viewing their art, hands pensively stroking their chins, trying to express their deep interpretations of the artists' inner moods.

STORY: Beauty is in the Eye

I presented some of my work in a small art show and was tickled by the response. At one point a group had gathered by a piece I had done, and was discussing my emotions. I knew that I had added a teardrop to the woman's veiled face because a small rhinestone had fallen off my daughter's jeans and I couldn't bear to throw it away. Instead, I stuck it on the cheek of the woman in my painting. I liked it. A patron decided, however, that I was deeply sad and moved to express myself through this third party, the woman in my painting. How 'bout that? I really wanted to jump up and down, smiling to reassure her that I was fine and explain that the rhinestone had just fallen on the floor and I stuck it on my painting with Elmer's glue. But I didn't. Actually, I was touched to see those people take the time to consider who might be behind the work and to allow their minds to ponder what the images meant to them.

Ganim and Fox, Guides we encountered earlier on our journaling stop, are also featured guests here, on our art walk. They state, "Artists have long known intuitively what research now confirms—that creating a visual image can produce physical and emotional benefits for both creator and viewer." The ability to change our emotional selves, as well as our physical bodies, can be achieved through the use of imagery.

Ganim introduces us to Dr. Gilah Yelin Hirsch.[66]

JOURNEY GUIDE

Gilah Yelin Hirsch

Los Angeles artist and professor who painted her way through understanding and healing from a paralysis that affected her entire left side.

Hirsch, at the age of ten, wanted to know if there were a God, so she wrote to Albert Einstein to ask. He answered her letter, advising her to form her own opinions. She has spent decades doing that. Her paintings reflect her Jewish heritage, interest in metaphysics and desire to be a catalyst for global harmony. Her artwork is often purchased by hospitals and medical facilities for its healing qualities. Hirsch works in a multidisciplinary manner including art, anthropology, architecture, theology, philosophy, psychology, psychoneuroimmunology and world culture.

To heal herself from her own afflictions, she gave shape, form and color to the horrific images she perceived within her body. She continued this process for one year, persistently regenerating the colors used until they were fertile images. The color green represented this energy. Following a revival of her soul, her paralysis disappeared and she is an internationally acclaimed artist and teacher.

Next we meet Betty Kjelson.[67]

JOURNEY GUIDE

Betty Kjelson

An artist who was burned while making her art and used color to heal herself.

The materials that Kjelson used in her art of making handmade paper from subtropical plants nearly killed her. She received second and third-degree burns on twenty-five percent of her body when boiling water spilled down her back and legs. She was given only a fifty-percent chance for survival. Using color to transfer her sensations and experience with pain, out of her body and on to the page, Kjelson encourages others to use art to heal.

Many artists have chronicled a healing journey through the gateway of artistic expression, whether it was to heal the fear of death, or as with Frida Kahlo, to portray the pain she experienced. Meinrad Craighead did transformational work through her art, in which she received integration, nourishment and a sense of wholeness. She is quoted as saying, "Memories ripen within us, heated by the imagination. We shape them into pictures or poems or music, words or dance. We animate what we draw up from the heart—thus giving shape to our own unique stories."

Mexican-born artist, Frida Kahlo[68] speaks to us of her pain and her art.

JOURNEY GUIDE

Frida Kahlo

Following an accident, she painted mostly self-portraits; depicting her pain, miscarriages and sexuality. She was married to famous artist Diego Rivera.

Kahlo contracted polio as a child which left one leg withered. She hid it with colorful skirts. Then, as a young adult, she was on a bus that collided with a trolley car. She was impaled on an iron handrail that penetrated her abdomen and uterus. She suffered additional injuries that included a broken spinal column, ribs, pelvis, collarbone, crushed leg and foot and dislocated shoulder. She lay in bed, in a body cast for many years. During that time, she propped a mirror and canvases and painted portraits of herself that depicted her physical and psychological pain.

The transcendent stories of sixteen artists, including some of those mentioned above, are featured in a book titled, *Artist's of the Spirit.* They have used their art to heal through their traumas and encourage others to do the same.

In recent years, studies have focused on how the right and left sides of the brain operate. There's conclusive evidence that people think in images, rather than words. To paraphrase Ganim's research, this is the process: Perceptions are first subconscious and cellular. Then the right sides of our brains record our experiences and feelings in the form of sensory images. These are recorded as they occur, without judgments or thoughts, and then get stored as image memories. Our right brains process these images and our feelings move to the left side of the brain. There, they're put into categories, analyzed and judged in order to fit our emotions. So many important experiences occur for us when we are preverbal, and drawing can, literally, help to draw these experiences out of us.

STORY: Earthquake

I worked as a therapist in a family crisis unit in southern California and was part of a triage team comprised of medical doctors, psychiatrists, and therapists who were called in to deal with families experiencing trauma from natural disasters; specifically earthquakes.

In October of 1987, I was five months pregnant with our first child. The pregnancy only served to heighten my already amplified psychic sense. Around seven o'clock one morning, I awakened from a dream and shared it with my husband.

In the dream, we were experiencing an earthquake. From a higher perspective, I saw myself, still asleep in bed, and my husband, in the bathroom. The shaking woke me and, as we had practiced many times before, I moved to the doorway of our bedroom, where my husband met me. He, my protruding belly, and I, rode out the quake and were fine.

After listening to me, he said that he was glad that it had just been a dream, and went into the shower to get ready for work. I stayed in bed until approximately ten minutes later, when the earth began to shake. Almost robotically, I moved to the doorway where he met me, still in his towel. We rode out the quake and were fine.

Later in the day, the call came to report to the center. We saw families shaken up emotionally, as well as physically, by the earthquake. I was incredibly calm during this one because I had been given the precognitive heads-up.

One therapist was assigned to the adult caregivers of each family, while another saw the children. I worked with the children. They drew monsters under the ground that pushed up dirt, along with their houses. They sketched large teeth chomping through the earth from below. There were ocean cities, underground, in which waves rose beneath their neighborhoods.

We experienced some aftershocks while they were there, and they drew some more. The families were educated about what an earthquake really is, we had some cookies and juice, and we all went home.

It wasn't until a week or so later, that I was given a most unusual case. This family reported having been out of town during the quake. Their four-year old daughter, upon returning home, was suddenly fearful of water. She wouldn't drink it, wouldn't wash her face, bathe or brush her teeth. She also wouldn't use the toilet and had regressed to wetting and soiling the bed. Unwilling to speak about her fears, she ran, shrieking, when anyone turned on the faucet. After several days, the parents called the center for help.

I met this adorable little girl and asked if she would like to draw pictures with me. Very happy to do that, she said she didn't want talk about what scared her. Her parents told her she'd have to talk about that to me and she cried. I assured her that we could just draw for the time being. We chatted about Barbies, stickers, and her favorite stories, while we drew.

Each of us had our own sheet of paper and I invited her to draw whatever she wanted to draw. She used the crayons to create her home in colorful detail. Flowers were as tall as the house and there was lots of green grass and a swing set.

One of the boys, who had been drawing with another therapist, got up to wash his hands and suddenly, this calm little girl stood, grabbed a red crayon and zig zagged it across her page, then on to mine, before seizing both papers, ripping them and squeezing them into a ball. She flew into my arms and sobbed.

I held her for a few moments and then gave her a fresh piece of paper and asked her to draw what scared her. A number of vicious looking sharks, leaping out of faucets, buckets, the toilet and the pool appeared. She was trembling when she completed her drawing. I held her again, and asked her to tell me about the drawing. She said, "Since we got back, they keep talking about the *aftersharks*." Ohh. In her dear mind, aftersharks, rather than aftershocks, followed earthquakes, and she figured that if she could just avoid water then she'd be safe.

Her family was brought back into the room, with their therapist, and I explained her perceptions. Once she understood, she was happy again. The family let us know the next day, that all had returned to normal. Even when she experienced subsequent aftershocks, she was not concerned.

I wish that all traumas were resolved that easily.

Your invitation to create art can invoke your dragon, but it can also touch your inner child and help him or her heal. Imagine what might have happened had this sweet girl's family not brought her in and had forced her to behave differently. That happens all of the time.

For many unconscious reasons, there are strong reactions to being asked to make colorful marks on a page. But even giving permission to go out of the lines can sidestep your Dragon and be very freeing. I invite you to do just that. Doodling is also an enchanting and stress-reducing activity.

Betty Edwards[69] encourages us to draw the inner artist out.

JOURNEY GUIDE

Betty Edwards

Artist, painter, teacher and author of Drawing on the Right Side of the Brain.

Edwards did split-brain research and found that the two hemispheres of the brain have different functions. Her drawing exercises bring out the creative abilities of the right side of the brain, as opposed to the analytic and logical abilities of the left brain. Critical Dragon is forced to sit in the corner, thumb in mouth.

In our society, we are often taught to rely on our thoughts rather than our feelings. "Follow your head, not your heart." Belief systems can influence the verbal left brain, and so the filter used to decipher feelings may be tainted. In order to get to the true feelings, the right brain must be accessed through drawing or visualization or other forms of artistic expression. Then we must remember to keep up this practice of play.

Pablo Picasso said, "Every child is an artist. The problem is remaining an artist once he (or she) grows up."

Activities:

Art

1. **Think back to your childhood experiences with art. Who or what encouraged you? Who or what defeated and stifled you? Journal about your recollections.**
2. **What is the worst thing that Critical Dragon could say about your art? Consider some comebacks. Journal.**
3. **Put on some music and doodle for 15 minutes. Journal about how it felt and what you noticed about yourself and your doodles.**
4. **Switch hands and doodle with your non-dominant hand. What do you notice? (Yes, journal about it, with either hand.)**
5. **Close your eyes for a few moments and imagine that you already possess the skills, raw talent, materials and one-way ticket to Away for Critical Dragon, to create any piece of art, in any art form. What would it look like? Write it down. (Put it in your Sprout file.) Better yet, create the art.**
6. **Ah. Key #8 is yours.**

Action Plan:

Decide upon ways that you can invite art into your daily life. Remember, you don't necessarily have to make art. You *are* art. You can consider going to view art, notice art in architecture, or appreciate the art created by Mother Nature. It's all around you. Just let it in.

Chapter Thirteen: Nature

Key #9

Realign yourself with the beauty and serenity of the natural world.

At this stop, I encourage you to take off your shoes. Let the grass tickle your soles and squish the earth between your toes.

The cultivation of reverence for nature allows your internal and external worlds to be joined. Chief Seattle, the Native American man who wrote to the President of the United States and asked him to consider the point of view from the American Indian's perspective, reminds others of the importance of quiet observation of nature and connection to all living things.

There is no quiet place in (your) cities, no place to hear the leaves of spring or the rustle of insects wings…The Indians prefer the soft sound of the wind darting over the face of the pond, the smell of the wind itself cleansed by a midday rain, or scented with pinion pine. The air is precious to the red man, for all things share the same breath—the animals, the trees, the man. Like a man who has been dying for many days, a man in your city is numb to the stench.

Shake off the habits that have made you numb to the natural glory around you. All of us have become caffeine-fueled, processed, fast-forwarded and mail-merged into oblivion. We've lost touch with the rhythms of nature and the natural laws of the universe. How sad and unhealthy this is for us and for our future generations.

Lean on a tree. Remember those simpler times as a child. What comes up for you? I recall making "tea," for my outdoor tea parties, by rubbing tree parts between my fingers so the tiny seeds fell into my sun-faded green teapot. I also pretended that a simple rock I'd found, turned out to be solid gold and then I'd daydream about what I'd do with my riches.

Sit still for a moment, allow your breathing to quiet and invite all of your senses to awaken. Let your thoughts wander back to those unencumbered times. In your mind, go to a favorite nature spot of your childhood. Everyone has one of some sort. Walk around there and feel your spirit release.

Now bring your awareness to today. Notice if your body tenses. When was the last time you watched the sun rise or set, listened to birds or tree frogs, or slowed the blur of your life down enough to breathe deeply? If you don't know when the last time was that you were perfectly healthy yet stayed in your night clothes during the day and cuddled with loved ones or pets, then it's been too long. When did you last create the opportunity to allow the day to unfold, rather than forcing it into the confines of an overstuffed calendar?

Time designated for birthday parties, deadlines, religious school, sports, music, art lessons, and carpooling, needs to be shared with time spent meandering in a field, strolling in the woods or by a stream, smelling flowers or pressing the leaves of herbal plants between your fingers to explode their scents. Some more of that time is supposed to be spent sleeping. We don't do enough of that, either. No wonder we're stressed!

Even those of us who have made a conscious effort not to over schedule our children and to be discerning about where we place our own time and energy, can find ourselves yelling, "Come on, kids. We have one hour and thirty-five minutes to get out there and commune with nature, damn it. Quit dragging your feet!"

Before you can be granted the Nature key, you must learn to say "no." This is an important skill. It's very challenging and easier said than done. If you're like me, you don't like to disappoint people. Critical Dragon jumps on that opportunity with both scaly feet and bears down with full weight. How can you say no to making cookies all afternoon for the school's bake sale, because you want to sit in the garden and watch the butterflies instead? Learn to, sometimes.

"Lazy" and "non-productive" are nasty names that Critical Dragon calls you when it's time to play dirty---which for Critical Dragon is all of the time. Even if you were to sit in the garden and watch the butterflies, Critical Dragon would abuse you if you weren't also at least pulling weeds. What kind of slouch just sits in the garden and enjoys the beauty of nature? Worthless sloth.

Guess what? Your External Enchantress is here to remind you that you deserve to sit in the garden. In doing so, you are honoring the beauty of creation. You'll be a better mother or father, wife or husband, woman or man, therapist or whatever you do in the world, for having done this.

Typically, fine, upstanding, responsible people like yourself get sidetracked on your way out to the garden. Laundry baskets full of dirty clothes call to you. Lush garden vs. stinky socks. Seems like it'd be an easy call. Not so.

"Finish your chores before going out to play!"
(When Dragons mock our mothers it is a low blow.)
Remember the Lemmejust Dragon? Lemmejust do a load of wash and then I'll sit in the garden and relax. What if this happened to you? Would you be able to ward off the Lemmejust Dragon and put the laundry aside while you sat idly in paradise? Surprisingly you might not be able to do it.

What about a compromise? You could put one load in and then stroll out to the garden while it washed. You could take the basket of clean clothes outside and fold them in the fresh air.

When you can feel your full breath return to your lungs, you know you've reached a solution that brings you peace. For years I chose the responsible route: my chores. If there was not time for the sit-n-stare in the garden, oh well. But guess what? There was never time. Eventually I realized that I had to trick myself into believing that I would be even better, more efficient, more loving, if I could do things that my soul longed to do.

Even though it's absolutely true that you are better when you honor those longings, it's not scripted into our upbringing. That was framed as "selfish," in the old days. These days, we need to change the meaning of "selfish" to what it is, "for the self," so that we can feel nourished and refreshed, in order to be able to share ourselves with others. Being self-centered used to carry the worst connotation of single minded, hedonistic purpose in living out only one's desires in a myopic view of life. Think, for a moment, of how nice it would be if we were all a little more self-centered, as in centered with the self. One of the paths back to inner peace can be found by aligning ourselves with nature. We find our internal balance when we sleep on an issue, walk with it in nature, and commune with our overworked, beaten up souls.

Austrian philosopher, literary scholar, educator, artist, playwright, and social thinker, Rudolph Steiner[70] joins us.

JOURNEY GUIDE

Rudolph Steiner
Founder of anthroposophy, Waldorf education, biodynamic agriculture, and anthroposophical medicine.

Children who attend the Waldorf Schools learn to appreciate and revere nature. Anthroposophy is a path of knowledge that guides the spiritual in the human being to the spiritual in the universe, which is an important component of the Waldorf education philosophy. Biodynamic agriculture is a form of organic farming practice that includes the relationships among the plants, the earth and the farmers. Anthroposophical medicine refers to medical practitioners who follow Steiner's teachings. A principle concept of good health lies in the connection with nature and the nurturing of our souls.

Rahima Baldwin [71] meanders along the trail.

JOURNEY GUIDE

Rahima Baldwin
Author and Waldorf School educator who understands the importance of letting children feel the textures of the earth in their toys and surroundings.

In her book, *You Are Your Child's First Teacher,* Baldwin points out that the toys most children come in contact with these days are made of plastic. Mirroring Steiner's beliefs, Baldwin supports the idea that children need exposure to toys made of natural fibers, such as wooden rattles and bowls of brightly colored yarn.

On your journey to reconnection with nature, you might gather items to display on a nature table. Please be sure not to disturb nature in doing so. You wouldn't want to remove a nest that is only temporarily uninhabited, for instance. But picking up leaves or pinecones, discarded bird feathers or seed pods can make lovely additions to your nature table.

Ours is at the entryway of our home and I have one in my office, but you might choose another location for yours. There is a natural rhythm to changing it seasonally, but you could certainly add to it at any time. I like to display these seasonal inspirations on an inexpensive, half round, three-legged accent table, draped with one to two yards of fabric that coordinate with the seasons. Tones of gold and bronze can be used for the fall table one year and for the sandy beach and sun of summer, another year. Green shades are nice for spring and blues and purples for winter. A white cloth with brown bark, red cardinal feathers and holly berries also make a nice winter scape. Please use your imagination and have fun creating this enchanting space.

Whether you decorate the table along with children, or do this as a solo activity, it's an opportunity to go on a gathering walk. On the first day of the solstice or equinox, you can dress the table and have a ceremony that acknowledges the changes that have occurred and foretells of the dreams for the next season; what you will metaphorically reap or sow.

For years I transformed the table on the eve of the solstice or equinox so that when the children came down in the morning they would be greeted with a new scene, reminding them of the change of seasons. We can't always rely on the weather to do that.

To foster further enchantment, you might designate a space in a closet or pantry for seasonal props. It's nice if nature tables contain natural elements but I must admit that I have added the occasional faux feathered bluebird from the craft store or fake butterfly to the mix.

In our home, we have four containers in which we store some staple items, each marked with the name of the season. For winter there are pinecones, some scented with cinnamon or pine oil, bare branches, and bird feathers that we have collected. (One year, our children added a freshly made snowball to the table. Within the hour it was appropriate for a summer water scene, but it was sweet to have them add their own touch to the creation.)

For spring, we have a tiny birdhouse and seed packets. In autumn, there are acorns that the children collected when they were small, along with special leaves and rocks we add to the table. Once, one of the decorations my youngest daughter added, walked away from the table when a snail shell, thought to be unoccupied, turned out to be inhabited. We found him and escorted him back outside to his real home.

The summer table is sprinkled with sand, to which a touch of white, shimmering glitter has been added. It offers great theatrical effect.

Gather different items and be mindful of what you add so that the table evolves each time and is never the same. You might keep a photo album of your nature scapes. Hold the principles of reduce, reuse and recycle as another way to honor nature. Beyond our responsibility to treat the earth with reverence and awe, is our duty to leave a place lovelier than when we found it. The Girl and Boy Scouts of America practice this principle. We need to teach others how to treat Mother Earth and then live the example.

Anything that you can do to attract wildlife, while caring to preserve it, is also effective. Birdbaths, bird feeders, butterfly bushes and toad abodes (as simple as a terra cotta flower pot on its side with some water pooling in it) all call nature to your door, but it's up to you to feed, clean, and tend these spaces. There's minimal work involved, but the rewards are rich and endless.

One summer we swapped out our old hummingbird feeder, to a store collecting and donating them to schools, for one that attaches by suction cups to the window. We placed it outside of our dining area. It was amazing to watch these tiny creatures light on the feeder, drink the nectar through their needle-sized beaks and then leave, like small hovercrafts. It's better than any television show.

Stargazing can be another bonding family activity. Even the addition of wind chimes to your porch or deck can bring the music of the earth to your home. Wind chimes make a lovely wedding or housewarming gift and the recipients usually don't get duplicates. Have fun as you find new means to include nature in your way of thinking and being in the world.

Modern technology has made so many chores easier for us that it's hard to believe that a common complaint is that we don't have enough time to do the things we want to do. People always tell me that they desire a connection with nature but just don't have the time. Why? What are we doing that keeps us so busy and off balance? Part of the answer may lie in this technological age.

Sit down on the earth and think about the rhythms of the day. Notice that the sun comes up in the east and sets in the west. The clouds get full and it rains. The seasons change. Like it or not, time marches along, on its path. Our ancestors awakened with the sun. They did their work until dark, cleaned their bodies, ate and went to sleep shortly after that.

Things are very different today. Our sun shines according to our preference for which way we spin our dimmer switches on our Halogen light fixtures. We are dry when it rains because of wood, sheet rock or other materials that shield us from the elements, and we are warm or cool because of artificially controlled temperatures in our environments. Let's pause for a moment of silent reflection and gratitude for modern conveniences. Many people move through each day without even noticing these things, never mind the daily phenomenon in nature that occurs; unless, of course, they inconvenience us. Let a soccer game get rained out and rescheduled during a ballet recital and all hell breaks loose.

The Internet, a connector in many ways, is also a time-sucker and isolator. Hours pass by unnoticed while on the computer. Electronics have often replaced what might otherwise be opportunities to go outside, connect with others, or rest.

Jane Roberts [72] offers guided views about the use of rest and waking time.

JOURNEY GUIDE

Jane Roberts

Trance channeler through whom the Seth material was received.

Roberts wrote about our disconnected society, in which we stay up for long periods of time and then try to sleep for one long one, each night. It's suggested that we would be better off if we napped midway through the day. We'd be balanced and connected with our spiritual guides, who can communicate with us more easily when we are not distracted by the events of living. While engaged in the alpha brain wave levels, or during deeper sleep, we can experience our inner wisdom, return to our waking lives refreshed, and with a renewed perspective. Various cultures support mid-day "siestas" and long, lunch breaks.

Naps are nice. Babies get to take them but if most of us nap, we feel guilty. We're naughty and decadent or others try to make us feel that way. Usually, we're interrupted by concerned people who are so unaccustomed to seeing us in a horizontal position that they rouse us to be sure that we haven't died.

Babies have the right idea, though. If you've ever watched one, you know that there are distinct rhythms that vacillate between levels of waking activity and alertness and periods of sleep or decreased mental and physical activity. Babies, according to their own individual schedules, let us know that they want to eat when they are hungry, be changed when they are wet, and kept at a comfortable temperature for their little, individual thermostats. That seems to be okay for a while, but in most cases, there is a rude awakening and the baby has to conform to a schedule that works for others in his or her environment. We all seem to adjust, but let's not forget about that frog that allowed himself to be boiled to death. The point is that we need to remember how to tune in to our inner rhythms, our environments, and nature, in order to recalibrate ourselves.

Several years ago, I had the urge to gather people together to acknowledge the change of seasons, but didn't know how. The synchronicity was not lost on me when, in the period of a year, I met three different Native American women, under three different circumstances, all belonging to the Lakota tribe. Each of them shared her rituals with me and I have continued to practice several of them.

One such gift of awareness was learning to honor the change of seasons during the spring and autumn equinox and summer and winter solstice. At times I've held large community celebrations and, at other times, have gathered together with an intimate group of family and friends. We bring poetry, art, and gifts from nature, along with some food to nourish the others present. You might want to try your hand at hosting a celebration of the season. It can be as elaborate or as simple as you wish.

Dragon Alert!

Your dragon doesn't think you need to host a seasonal celebration. In that case, let me share with you how to do it so ol' party pooper doesn't put the kibosh on your plans.

How to Host a Solstice/Equinox Celebration

1. *Invitations.* Send invitations or call those with whom you'd like to share this celebration. The dates are marked on most calendars as the First Day of Autumn or the First Day of Summer, etc. Invite them to dress comfortably and appropriately for the weather. Try to hold the ceremony part outside if possible. Ask them to bring food to share with the other guests. You may also need them to bring a towel or chair to sit on as well.

2. *Yarn Circle.* A yarn circle is taken from a Native American birthing ritual. A skein of multi-colored yarn is wound in front of and behind each person in the circle until it arrives back at the first person. Pass a knife or scissors and snip the yarn from the person on your left and then ask them to tie the yarn around your wrist. This is symbolic of cutting the cord that makes us individuals, but reminds us that, as we carry the colors of our neighbor's yarn as well, we are all connected.

3. *Elements of Nature.* Participants can bring elements of nature, such as gourds, pumpkins, leaves, pinecones, shells, flowers, fruit or bird feathers or you can have already gathered them yourself. (Try to avoid the Moon and Stars birthday party syndrome. This should be fun for you, too.) If you like, the gathering can include a nature hike to collect the elements right then. Remember that nature should never be disturbed for this purpose but there are always many offerings available. Place these items at a central spot and then be seated in a circle around them.

4. *Art.* Hand out paper and pencils or crayons, along with a sturdy surface to lean on, such as a magazine or piece of cardboard. You might want to accompany this activity with music or simply enjoy the sounds of nature. Then, using your non-dominant hands, draw the elements. (Expect loud dragon noise here.) Some people choose one item and lose themselves in the details while others may loosely sketch the shapes of the entire arrangement. It serves to literally draw your focus inward to the essence of the season. Also, because it is the non-dominant hand, dragon chatter is quieted because expectations are very low.

5. *Movement.* If you have the right crowd (meaning each individual didn't invite his or her Critical Dragon) then you can put on some mood music or Native American selections and move your bodies to nature's rhythm of the season; whether it's falling leaves or seedlings sprouting from the ground.

6. *Drumming Circle.* This drumming circle takes place as you transition into the Medicine Wheel. Natural instruments, such as rattles or gourds with dried seeds inside, drums or rain sticks (which can be paper towel holders filled with uncooked rice and sealed on each end) are selected. You can move in a circle, calling in the spirits of the animals, the ancestors, the four directions, Grandmother Earth and Grandfather Sky. Then those energies are brought down through your bodies to make yourselves a conduit between earth and sky and all that there is in between.

7. *Medicine Wheel.* Participants sit in a circle and the leader points out which way is north, east, south, and west. Then each person is asked to silently choose an issue that is challenging at the time. Note: With larger groups it is easier to visualize walking around the circle and stopping at each of the directions, while remaining seated. For smaller groups, all can actually walk it together

or take turns. The wheel is "walked," through all of the directions, each associated with an animal spirit. You would begin by visualizing yourself at the center of the circle. The east is first, overseen by the Golden Eagle. The issue is observed from a different perspective as you fly above your usual vantage point.

Back to the center, you move next to the south, governed by the Red Coyote. Red Coyote howls at you and turns things upside down. If you've been taking yourselves too seriously, the howls are an invitation to lighten up and laugh, breathe, or rethink issues. If, on the other hand, you've been taking situations too lightly you may hear yelps as warnings to pay attention.

Another perspective has been added as you move back to the center and then toward the west, and the position of the Black Bear. The Black Bear represents the darkness or the shadow side that hibernates. It's also a popular hangout for Critical Dragon. Dragon emerges from the cave. Fear, loneliness, and difficult feelings or issues are explored here.

You move back to the center, then to the north and the White Buffalo. White Buffalo represents illumination. Emerging from the darkness, you step into the light. The return to the center each time serves to ground you in your new wisdom, piece by piece.

If any other creatures have visited during your ceremony, and several always do, even when you're inside, you include their animal medicine as well. You close with a blessing for those who need healing of one sort or another and for peace. Then you can share a meal to which each of you has contributed.

Following, there is most often a peaceful calm. Each person leaves with a sense of renewal and focus for the season ahead.

This kind of ritual is especially helpful with transitions and people who find change challenging. It doesn't matter if you celebrate the passing of seasons in a group or alone, or whether there is a variance in weather during the seasons at all. This acknowledgement creates a powerful connection to nature.

In case your Dragons suggest that it's too hard to do, here's a quick list of everything you might need to pull off a celebration like this:

1. Invitations
2. A skein of multi-colored yarn
3. A knife or scissors
4. Elements of Nature (gather acorns, shells, etc.)
5. Paper
6. Something to lean on while drawing
7. Pencils or crayons
8. Music (optional)
9. Establish beforehand which way is north, east, south and west. For the Medicine Wheel you may wish to learn more by gathering resources beforehand.

Activities:

Connection to Nature

1. **For one weekend, or longer, attune yourself to the rhythms of the day. What do you observe about yourself?**
2. **Create a nature table or clear a space in which to honor nature. Bring in elements that reflect the season.**
3. **Reduce, Reuse, Recycle. Beyond what you may already do, go through your closet, your pens, etc. to see where else you may put the three Rs into practice.**
4. **Take a look at what takes you away from nature. What wastes the majority of your time? Is**

it time spent on the computer, reading junk mail, surfing the net, texting, talking on the phone? You may find that it involves an electronic device. If so, replace that with a connection to nature.

5. **For twenty minutes a day, immerse yourself in the sights, sounds, smells, and even tastes of nature.** Lie on your back and look up at the sky, the clouds, or the stars. Sit against the base of a tree or by a stream. Smell herbs or flowers in a garden, or watch the birds.
6. **Host an equinox/solstice celebration!**
7. **Sit outside with your new key, #9.**

Action Plan:

Discover the various ways that you can invite nature into your conscious awareness and everyday routine. Read the paper and sip your tea or decaffeinated coffee outside, and air out your spirit. List the places you can visit, both near and far, that nurture your connection to our Mother Earth. The list gives you a reference point of places to go when you notice that your buzz is coming from the electromagnetic frequency given off by the equipment surrounding you. Make connection to nature a part of every day.

Chapter Fourteen: Meditation

Key #10

This is another rest stop. Relax.

I could talk to you about meditation, but there would be nothing to say. It's like discussing silence. What an oxymoron. Yet there are many teachers of meditation who speak volumes about the historical information and research on the healing effects of meditation. Some of them will join us in a moment. Their valuable resources in the field of healing and stress management, along with others, can be found in the bibliography.

Please know that there are numerous ways to meditate. You need not roll up like a pretzel to quiet your mind. Meditations can include walking, writing, singing, and breathing.

Critical Dragon can get pretty loud in the silence. As a matter of fact, let's do a Dragon Check-in right now. See what your Critical Dragon has to say about meditation.

"What a waste of time!"

I thought so. That's a popular phrase for Critical Dragon to spew. You might also be accused of trying to justify escape. For now, pick a spot, sit down and find a comfortable, relaxed posture. Take a few deep and cleansing breaths in through your nose and release through your mouth. Roll your shoulders a few times, then your head. You're getting very good at this. You may close your eyes at any time.

Track your breath, in and out. Don't work to alter it right now. Just follow the rhythm of this life-sustaining process. Envision some restorative place of peace and beauty. It may be one that already exists, somewhere that you've been or have heard about, or a sanctuary of your own imagination. Picture yourself there and in your mind turn around in a circle, 360 degrees, all the way around.

Take in the sights of this sacred space. Notice the colors that are present. If you can see the sky, observe how it changes. What is the temperature? Climate? Season? What time of day is it?

Let the overlay of sounds enter your awareness. What are your favorite sounds in this place?

And the smells. What scents do you connect with there?

Add another layer with the tastes linked to where you are; even if it's only the taste of the air.

Notice the textures; their contrasts and similarities. Appreciate their unique qualities.

Become aware of how your spirit feels. And breathe. Breathe. Breathe.

We'll let the Guides surround us and share their wisdom about the various benefits to practicing the art of meditation. They form a long parade line, with many more following behind. Just rest and open yourself to experience a snippet of what each has to offer.

OM, here's Rice again. He traces the history of meditative practices to Hindu literature, and portrays it as the road to enlightenment, as was sacrifice ↑end prayer. The intention of meditation, often combined with yogic practice, was to withdraw from illusions and mesh with the Oversoul.

Edmund Jacobson[73] approaches.

JOURNEY GUIDE

Edmund Jacobson

American physician who developed Progressive Muscle Relaxation (PMR) in the 1920's. He noted the connection between muscle tension and anxiety and concluded that teaching people to relax their muscles would lead to decreased anxiety.

PMR has been used successfully to treat migraines, tension headaches, hypertension, insomnia, test anxiety, performance anxiety, flight phobias and Raynaud's disease. Subsequent clinicians began to teach the technique to patients so they weren't in need of a facilitator in order to achieve the results.

Variations of this process had begun to be used for stress management. These include autogenic therapy, Transcendental Meditation, Benson's Relaxation Response, and hypnosis.

Johannes Schultz.[74] joins us.

JOURNEY GUIDE

Johannes Schultz

German psychiatrist who developed autogenic training, in 1932, as a relaxation technique. Autogenic, meaning "self-produced," is a way of maintaining the internal psychophysiological balance of the body.

The main objective of this process is to develop a relationship between thought and a calm state in the physical body. This is a state that Critical Dragon abhors.

Breathe deeply and rhythmically while you continue to release tension from your muscles and nerves. As each Guide joins our circle, take another breath and release; deepening your relaxation.

Way back when, there were nay-sayers about the benefits of meditation. Science overlapped with yogic practice when concrete physical evidence of the mind-body connection was desired. The ancient yogis claimed that they could alter their heart rate, change their body temperature, fire walk, penetrate the skin with a needle without bleeding, and change their consciousness.

Therese Brosse enters our circle.[75]

JOURNEY GUIDE

> # Therese Brosse
>
> *A French cardiologist who traveled through India in 1935, and carried a portable electrocardiograph to scientifically record the claims of these yogis. Her findings brought some merit to their claims.*

Also here are M.A. Wenger, B.K. Bagchi and B.K. Anand.[76]

JOURNEY GUIDES

> # Wenger, Bagchi & Anand
>
> *They followed in Brosse's path and discovered that the ability to regulate heart processes was achieved through muscular control and breath.*

Breathe.
Joseph Wolpe,[77] a South African psychiatrist offers his contribution.

JOURNEY GUIDE

> # Joseph Wolpe
>
> *He developed Systematic Desensitization in the 1950s to treat phobias, obsessive compulsive and other anxiety disorders.*

Systematic desensitization is a classical Pavlovian conditioning. If you were to utilize this technique, you'd learn relaxation skills first, to help you control your fear and anxiety with regard to specific phobias. Then you would establish a hierarchy of fears and overcome each one in steps.

Most people try to avoid situations or sources of fear to reduce their anxiety. With systematic desensitization, rather than moving away or avoiding what freaks you out, you get to imagine moving closer to it—easiest step to hardest—until the final step is overcome. The fear or anxiety is paired with the relaxation response until the relaxation is the response achieved.

So, as you imagine a fun-sucking dragon outside of your window, (the stimulus) you immediately breathe deeply, relax your muscles, imagine a place of safety or of peace, (removal of the stimulus) to extinguish the fear or anxiety. "Augh!" from the stimulus, is immediately paired with "Ahhh," the relaxation response.

Next is Maharishi Mahesh Yogi.[78] The Beatles were originally instrumental with his introduction to the United States.

JOURNEY GUIDE

> # Maharishi Mahesh Yogi
>
> *Brought Transcendental Meditation (or TM) to Western society. It gained popularity in the 1960's.*

This adaptation of Mantra Yoga was made a secular practice when the Maharishi eliminated elements he considered unnecessary. The practice of TM seemed to be shrouded in mystery and ceremony. It involved three sessions that included initial instruction, deeper instruction with the commitment to practice, and an initiation ceremony, during which one was given a mantra.

A mantra is a secret word or phrase that is not to be told to anyone. Most often, a meditation teacher or leader chooses a mantra specifically for each individual student. From that point on, the person practices alone, using repetition of the mantra as a focal point. It's then practiced 20-30 minutes per day, twice a day, usually just prior to breakfast and before dinner.

Since the secrecy surrounding the mantra seems like fertile breeding ground for dragons, I checked into what the consequences might be if someone did share his or her mantra with another.

Dr. Patricia Carrington[79] enlightens us about mantras.

JOURNEY GUIDE

> # Patricia Carrington
>
> *Professor, author and originator of Clinically Standardized Meditation (CSM); the training method used in medical institutions and other organizations. She is also the originator of (Emotional Freedom Techniques) EFT Choices Method, the advanced EFT method used worldwide by psychotherapists and trainers.*

According to Carrington, if you disclose your mantra to anyone, there won't be a lightning strike but the integrity of the association with the mantra would likely be diluted.

It sounds to me that for some, the initial admonition given with the mantra was warned in such an ominous way that people didn't question what might happen if…they just vowed to keep it private. Some believe that if revealed to another, the effect of the entire practice would be ruined.

More than admonition, at least in its roots in India, the mantra was a sacred gift given from teacher to student as a connection and commitment to their spiritual work together.

In psychological terms, as Carrington explains, if the word is revered as a repeated association or call to go inward and then is used casually in conversation, it's no longer reserved as a sacred heralding that automatically centers through conditioned response. So the effect of the mantra itself is diminished.

"Darn it! Way to ruin the mystery and steal my power!"
Herbert Benson[80] approaches.

JOURNEY GUIDE

Herbert Benson

An American born cardiologist and pioneer in the field of Mind-Body Medicine, he brought spirituality to healing and focused on the relaxation response as an antidote to the negative effects of stress.

Benson's Relaxation Response follows a four-step process: 1) A quiet environment, 2) A mental device, 3) A passive attitude and 4) A comfortable position.

1) A quiet environment removes distractions.

2) A mental device offers a focus away from the logical, thinking mind to a stimulus of a repetitive sound or word, which can be repeated aloud or silently. Concentration can also be fixed on an object, such as a flickering candle flame.

3) A passive attitude allows distracting thoughts to be acknowledged, but then the focus is gently guided back to the mental device, without judgment. (Note to self: Lock Critical Dragon in the bathroom before beginning.)

4) The physical position should be comfortable, without muscle tension. Lying down positions are often too sleep-inducing and it's believed that the original postures of sitting cross-legged, kneeling or swaying were used in order to prevent people from falling asleep while trying to meditate.

Benson initially believed that meditation was so powerful that just practicing it was enough to heal an individual. After years of working with people, he realized that the process is even more potent and healing when it contains a personal vision. This is the picture in your mind of what your ideal image of yourself is, whether it refers to vitality and good health, an emotional state of joy, or the experience of serenity.

Breathe. Did you remember to do that without my suggestion?

Kabat-Zinn returns to share more of his knowledge of meditation practice with us.

The Body-Scan Meditation is a technique that focuses on different parts of the body in a progression. Attention is given to each part, from the toes to the head, awareness is given to the sensations present, and then the breath is directed to each area. The process is slow and methodical and ends with the imagery of a whale's blowhole at the top of the head, through which energy flows down through the entire body and back up again.

Try it.

As we've discussed through the use of the Dragons, thoughts carry with them varying degrees of energy charges. Some are perceived as positive, some negative and others are neutral.

Kabat-Zinn teaches us that meditation allows a separateness that invites us to view these thoughts from a more detached perspective, so that all thoughts can be considered and given equal attention. This diminishes focus on the Dragonesque, highly charged, negative thoughts and brings wholeness to the experience; inclusive of all thoughts and emotions. When all thoughts and emotions are observed neutrally, with equal consideration, the negative thoughts and emotions lose their charge as being right or real for a person, and simply take their place alongside the others.

And breathe.

Bernie Siegel, who prefers just to be called, "Bernie," graces us with his presence again. His belief in empowering his patients so that they may live fully and die peacefully is paramount. You may remember his first book, *Love, Medicine and Miracles,* which redirected his life.

Siegel asserts that knowledge of the emotional self is necessary in order to assist the physical self with healing; especially in cooperation with a cancer. He also believes that gaining an understanding of ways in which love has been blocked is a key factor in the experience of healing, whether it resides in the capacity to receive love from the self or others, or in the ability to give. Meditation provides a route for this examination. In his work with cancer patients, he has encountered Dragons up close and personally. He uses what he calls, "carefrontation" to facilitate this change and healing through a loving, safe and therapeutic confrontation of the self.

Breathe and stretch.

Dacher reminds us that toxic pharmaceuticals and radiation therapy have been used extensively in the treatment of many cancers. Although the cancerous areas are under attack from the potent medication, so are all of the healthy areas of the system as well. The good news is that alternative mind-body therapy and self-regulating techniques, such as meditation, guided imagery, biofeedback and attitudinal healing, are beginning to be included in the treatment of cancer, in order to balance these negative effects.

These powerful techniques may be used by everyone. Clearing negative thoughts, shifting beliefs and replacing them with images of strength and healing can assist you on your path toward well-being in the body, mind, spirit and emotions.

Breathe.

Weil is back. He uses Interactive Guided Imagery as an effective mind-body therapy. It accesses the material in the unconscious mind to gain information about the origin of illness, as well as what is needed for healing. Weil openly reveals his personal study and experimentation in the field of altered consciousness, assisted by the use of many plant-based substances. He offers that the consciousness-altering drugs do not produce the high but rather open the body's ability to access those centers from within.

Weil has begun to look at aging from several perspectives; beyond the physical, that include the social and cross-cultural. He suggests that while the aging process cannot be reversed, it can be accompanied by good health, "serenity, wisdom, and its own kind of power and grace."

Dr. Robert Matusiak[81] a professor of mine, visits.

JOURNEY GUIDE

Robert Matusiak

A professor of psychology, researcher, and psychotherapist, who specializes in the field of trauma resolution.

One of the things he taught me was the importance of putting our traumas on the timeline of our experiences, as opposed to living as if they are continually occurring in the present. Imagine how invested Critical Dragon would be in keeping the experience of the trauma fresh, so you wouldn't be able to move past it. All of your decisions and reflections of yourself would be run by that trauma as if it were your power center. Decide not to give that power to Critical Dragon anymore.

One step toward putting your trauma in its rightful place is to quiet the automatic and mechanical mind of mind-talk and shift to mindfulness. The trauma is not occurring in the present moment. Through attention, concentration and meditation, we can develop an accurate and precise awareness of our minds, bodies, and outer world, and attain full health. Traumas, as well as milestones and celebrations, are all part of who we are and need to be lived through and then placed on the continuum of experience in our lives.

Dragon Alert!

"You're killin' me here!"

It wasn't until I became a board certified hypnotherapist that I learned, firsthand, how instrumental Critical Dragon has been in keeping people afraid of the word, "hypnosis." Dragons conjure images of control-crazy power-mongers who gain access to someone's private world, take control of their thoughts and lives. Some dragons will go so far as to whisper the words, "black magic" and "voodoo."

Hypnotherapy is a tool used to assist with the removal of a block or for the purpose of deep exploration. This kind of meditative state is most often facilitated by a professional; such as a licensed psychotherapist or psychiatrist, who have additional training in hypnosis. They are referred to as hypnotherapists. Paraprofessionals who perform hypnosis are called hypnotists. The requirements needed to add this skill to the practice of psychotherapy vary from state to state.

Your Enchantress has a bias that if you're trying to uncover unconscious material, it's best to consult professionals. Paraprofessionals, while able to access unconscious material in a trance state, may not be equipped to handle the emotion that can be released. Neither might they be able to recognize underlying psychological issues that may be present.

You can practice self-hypnosis. Guided imagery, walking, chanting, breathing to quiet yourself and drawing your attention inward are all paths to this form of meditation. It takes place in the alpha state, and we are in this trance-like place for three to four hours each day during our waking time. Any time that we're absorbed in reading a good book or are involved in performing a repetitive task, like washing dishes, that allows us to transcend our experience; we're in the alpha state.

You may recognize what it feels like to be in a trance state if you've driven yourself home, down a familiar path that you drive every day, without even recalling how you got there. That's the alpha state, which is optimum for meditation and for accessing the unconscious material. Delta, or deep sleep is too deep, and information isn't retrieved easily as when it's just below the surface. Beta levels include the chit-chatty patter that occurs most of the time.

Another deep and cleansing breath and release.

Carlson reassures us that meditation each day does not have to be three hours long. Twenty to thirty minutes, twice per day is ideal. You may do a writing meditation upon awakening and a walking meditation in late afternoon, or after dinner. Carlson worked in the field of stress management for several years, and observed that people who are inwardly peaceful carve out a little quiet, meditative time for themselves nearly every day. He suggests that the meditative time be spent during the practice of yoga, in nature, or anywhere that's away from the noise and pressures of life. He also references transitional times as opportunities to connect with one's self, such as before the start of the day, just prior to going to sleep, and on the way home from work.

I'm guessing that Happy Hours at local bars around the country gained popularity just trying to fill this niche. I don't recommend that, however. That kind of unconscious state is not what we're striving to achieve.

Carlson recommends that, after work, people drive on to their street, pull the car to the side of the road and sit quietly, observing the garden or the neighborhood, before entering the garage and house. He regards meditation as a significant path to both inner and outer peace, and believes that the experience of meditation allows such complete relaxation, that it teaches one how to be at peace in general.

Nhat Hanh, the monk who assisted us with mindfulness, likens the process of meditation to cloudy apple juice as it settles in a glass. He says, "You just sit…and the mind settles itself."

Eastman and Rozen, whose meditations are specifically designed for children, tell us that children can also easily learn to meditate. Their meditations help kids relate to things familiar in their world. There are the rag doll, birthday party, and the tense and release exercises.

Children imitate the rag doll; letting their limbs be limp and relaxed. The birthday party exercise uses breath, as if a deep breath were drawn and released to blow out candles on a birthday cake. Tense and release involves consciously tightening muscles and then releasing the tension, as in biofeedback techniques. This is useful in the treatment of anxiety and aggression.

This technique can also be taught in combination with a visualization tailored for each individual child. Children are invited to imagine a favorite character or sports figure as a positive role model. Then, while using the tense and release exercise, specifically to shift anxious or aggressive behavior, they imagine the role models performing the desired behavior and then adapt that behavior, themselves. Either a reward or consequence follows.

Breathe.

Rumi,[82] poet and mystic moves among us.

JOURNEY GUIDE

Mevlana Jalaluddin Rumi

He lived from 1207-1273 and was the founder of the sect known as Sufi Muslims. They achieved connection with God through trance dancing, as well as music, prayer, poetry, meditation, fasting and also self-flagellation or beating. The dancers in a form of Sufi dance ritual in Turkey are often referred to as "whirling dervishes."

A meditative state can be achieved by entrainment with a rhythmic pulse or synchronization with a sound. People, who perform religious rituals and ceremonies, as well as public speakers, use rhythm to induce a trance state. Research has shown that a particular kind of drumming can bring a group into a shared rhythm that is sacred. Shamanic practice uses drumming as a means of moving from one consciousness to another.

You can even use trance-inducing techniques to help your babies fall asleep. They often do that with their little heads resting on our hearts. Speaking rhythmically, at 45 beats per minute, mirrors the human heart rate at rest. So, if you are not holding them, but are speaking rhythmically to them while they are in their cribs, it can work.

Also, allowing them to fix their gaze on you and then slowly closing and opening your eyes can help to achieve the desired effect of getting babies to entrain with your quiet rhythms. Their eyes begin to open and close with yours. You then leave your eyes closed for longer and longer periods. Most often, they will do the same. You do run the risk, however, of falling asleep before they do. Please make sure that they are in a secure place before trying this exercise.

Moms and dads can benefit from achieving a meditative state. It's much trickier than being a mystic on the mountaintop. Anyone can meditate at the top of a quiet, snow-covered mountain. What's truly impressive is the mom or dad who, in the midst of chaos, can stop her or his anxiety, breathe deeply and be transported to a peaceful place while holding a teething baby as he or she begins a two-hour tirade.

"Yeah, you can't do that!"
Yes, you can!

Busy people always tell me that they don't have time to meditate or that their too-full minds wander. Let me demonstrate how I envision a Meditation for Busy People. It goes something like this: OOOOOOMMMMMMy goodness, I forgot to call the teacher! Breathe. Focus. OOOOOOMMMMMMy goodness, I didn't get milk! Breathe. Bring your thoughts back to your breath. OOOOOOMMMMMMMy goodness, I stink at meditation. Forget it!

Sound familiar? It is. And to most of us, since we are all the "busy people." On previous tours, participants expressed fear or failure regarding their attempts to meditate. Guests came up with the most creative reasons for not meditating. One man said he would, but just can't get comfortable in the lotus position since sustaining a football injury thirty years earlier. Another said that she doesn't have three hours a day to clear her time and her thoughts. Yet another was afraid that he'd fall asleep and snore. Several women were concerned that they might not be able to do it correctly. (Critical Dragon jumped all over that one and agreed.)

A young man told me that he used to "get in trouble for day dreaming" as a child. He was scolded repeatedly for wasting time, but now has reframed it as his "meditation time." He puts limits around it so he feels justified about allowing himself down-time in a way that feels comforting to him.

One woman feared that she'd be making herself susceptible to subliminal messages, although certainly none were being sent by me. I was too busy trying to impart the conscious ones. Another was worried that she might do something that would embarrass her. It was clear that their dragons were speaking over me. A few shared that they were not comfortable with their eyes closed. (If you're one of those people, and you want to keep your eyes open, that's just fine.) Dragons have a field day with meditation.

This is a friendly reminder that we don't want to slay our dragons. They do serve a purpose. But when it is to criticize us, thwart our positive efforts and bring harm, we can choose to ignore them. Sometimes, though, they are truly sending up signals to warn us about some impending concern.

In every case, your true inner voice is your best guide. If you're not comfortable doing something because the pit of your stomach tells you not to, then please do not do it. You can usually tell if you're stretching yourself to grow or to injury. If your gut tells you that something is not right for you then it doesn't matter if it's right for one hundred other people, don't do it. Maybe it's just the timing that isn't right or maybe it's the person facilitating it. The point is, listen to your inner voice. It's very wise. Practice so you can distinguish between your inner voice and that of Critical Dragon.

OM

Believed by some to be the original sound.

I thought I'd give you the brief 4-1-1 on the meaning of OM. It was believed that before the beginning of time, the Brahman, or absolute reality, was the one that was to become many. The vibration became sound; possibly the first sound and is considered the sound of vibration itself. The OM mantra represents moving through the stages of consciousness to perfect bliss, in which the self identifies with the Supreme Being. It sometimes is referred to as AUM, with the A embodying three stages of wakefulness, the U as the dream stage in between and the M, deep sleep. When OM is repeated, there is silence between them. The sound of OM is thought to be life-sustaining and runs through breath.

Chopra drops in on us again and says about meditation, "In the silent spaces between our thoughts, we communicate with our soul." He teaches Primordial Sound Meditation, during which a mantra is assigned. It has been mathematically calculated from the ancient Vedics from your birth time and place as the vibration created by the universe at the time of your birth.

A mandala is a universal symbol; a circle within the center of a circle. It appears in nature in Nautilus shells, fruit, rings on trees, and flowers. Labyrinths are a form of mandalas. They usually consist of concentric circles and are walked, as are Medicine Wheels, for the purpose of introspection and connection inward and outward. Tibetan Buddhists believe that a mandala consists of five "excellencies." They are: The teacher-The message-The audience-The site-The time. The audience, or viewer, is believed to be necessary to create the mandala. When there is no one to witness the mandala, it is said that there is no mandala. (This is akin to the tree falling in the woods and no one to hear it.)

A yantra is a cosmically inspired geometric design. The pattern may be drawn or occur naturally, as in a rose. By spending time gazing upon mandalas or yantras we are drawn within to greater realizations of esoteric qualities - beauty, truth, peace, and joy. In Yantra meditations, you stare at a brightly colored pattern of intricate geometric designs and that helps to balance the right and left sides of the brain.

Listening to meditation tapes that facilitate internal work can be very useful. They may contain guided visualizations or be a sound-track of meditative sounds that allow you to do what it is that you need to do. If you are sleep-deprived your meditation may turn into a power nap, because your body needs that. Meditating in this modern world can be tricky. To ensure that you don't "over meditate" (a.k.a. oversleep) you can set a watch alarm to sound five to ten minutes after the time you wish to return to present awareness. That can create greater freedom to get lost in the meditation, without fearing that you will meditate through a week's work and miss everything.

Some of my tour participants have expressed fear of getting into a meditation, or past-life regression, for that matter, and getting "stuck" there. I assure you that no one has ever left a tour wearing medieval boots when they came in with penny loafers, nor did they leave as Egyptian Princesses when they came in as administrative assistants. The good news, however, is that what they discovered about themselves during their meditations may have led to new haircuts or altered visions of how they could experience their lives.

Cameron catches up with us after she has walked prayerfully along. She reminds us that walking meditations break the rules on sitting still in the lotus position.

Dr. Barbra Fredrickson, Kimberly Coffey, Dr. Michael Cohn, and Dr. Jolynn Pek, with Dr. Sandra Finkel,[83] surround us to discuss loving-kindness meditations.

JOURNEY GUIDES

Fredrickson, Cohn, Coffey, Pek and Finkel

The research team, headed by Barbara Fredrickson, who studied the effects of positive emotions on our psychophysiology.

Fredrickson's "broaden-and-build" theory of positivity stockpiles positive emotions felt during daily experiences. The research team of Fredrickson, Cohn, Coffey, Pek and Finkel tested the outcome of performing loving-kindness meditations on these positive emotions and discovered that the building theory of adding on to the positive emotions created long term positive effects. The subjective experience of life became brighter, as did an increase in health and decrease in depression.

Loving-kindness meditations are gaining popularity. Focus is on flooding an individual, with love and/or experiencing the feeling of being flooded with love. Then, like the ripple effect from a pebble thrown into a pond, the circle of love or good wishes extends out wider and wider to encompass a country, world leaders, then the universe and all who inhabit it.

<u>Activities:</u>

<u>Meditation</u>

1. **Take a few moments for yourself. Relax, minimize distractions and breathe, deeply, in and out. Release the tension in your muscles and nerves, beginning with your feet and moving upward, toward your head. What is the first message that Critical Dragon throws up on your screen? Journal about it.**
2. **Experiment with different kinds of meditation, (e.g. sitting meditations, walking meditations, writing meditations, staring into the flame of a candle, meditations focusing only on breath or sound, ones that allow focus on a particular issue, ones involving nature) and record your experiences.**
3. **Create a sacred place of peace to go to in your meditations. You can fine-tune the images and change them each time you meditate. You may also begin your meditations from a sacred place of peace and journey from there and return to there before resuming your beta levels of functioning. Use all of your senses.**
4. **Close your eyes and prepare yourself to meditate. Experiment with a healing meditation. Invite Critical Dragon to go out for ice cream.** (This is like a circus for C.D.) **Choose a part of your physical body that may be holding tension. Imagine that that part of your body can separate itself from you to sit in front of you and speak to you. In your mind, dialog with it. Listen for what it says to you.** This is a Gestalt empty chair technique. **You may journal about this experience also.**

For instance, you may notice tension in your back. Breathe into it and ask your back to sit across from you. Ask it what its function is, when it's in balance. Your back might say that it holds you up and keeps all of the other parts connected. Consider whether you are being your back. Are you the backbone of the family, the office, the neighborhood, the Scout troop or the soccer parents? Do you feel responsible for keeping all of the other parts connected? If so, ask your back what created the tension. It will tell you.

It might say that it can support a lighter load but that you piled too much on it at one time. It may say that you have not allowed it to lie down in bed for long enough each night, or that it feels as though it's breaking in half because your dreams and desires of the upper regions are not being realized on the earth plane, under your feet. Ask your back, specifically, what it needs to return to balance. It might say that it needs someone else to share the load, or that you need to say "no" more often. Listen to it. Then actively hear what Critical Dragon (back from the ice cream parlor) has to say about it. If you don't, you may be surprised when C.D. sabotages your plans because you forgot that you're in charge of running the show.

5.   **Prepare yourself to meditate. As you rest and relax deeply, letting the tension release from your muscles and nerves, imagine yourself walking along a road or path. After awhile, notice the presence of an animal spirit who is there to meet you. What message does this animal spirit have for you? Connect with the message and thank the animal spirit for bringing it to you. Afterward, journal about the animal and the message received.** Also consider the animal and its unique characteristics. For example, if it is a bird, do you need to look at something from a higher perspective? If it is a hawk, how is that different from a dove? Consider all of the symbolism. If it's a mouse, think about how the mouse moves close to the ground, using whiskers as sensors. Mouse chews things to bits. Do you do that? Take in all of the information.

Action Plan:

Begin to work meditation time into each day. Start with fifteen minutes per day so that you don't become overwhelmed. Remember that you may combine activities to include this time, such as writing, doodling, walking. You may utilize it for the purpose of healing, setting an intention, goal or desire through focus or simply to recharge your battery.

By the way, you hold Key #10, to meditation, in your hand.

Chapter Fifteen

The Destination

Congratulations! You have arrived. I hope you are feeling energized and empowered, ready to roll up your sleeves and work/play toward reducing or eliminating your experience of stress in everyday life. My wish for you is that you are ready for enchantment and will make it a priority.

Step into the river wherever you are. Don't feel like you need to find the beginning or end. Just step in and keep moving. Recognize that you have choices and now tools, in your toolbox, to help make the job easier.

I know how overwhelming it can feel to go to the zoo or other amusement park. They give you that map that defines all of the areas of interest. When you begin, moving through each of those in one day seems very manageable. Each square inch may represent miles, but it appears to be about ten inches or so. No problem.

Then, halfway through the journey, you decide that you hate elephants and wouldn't look at a monkey if it dropped down in front of you! Taking a break and pacing yourself may ease it for you and keep you entertained.

So it is with *The Enchanted Journey*. Consider that you have an open pass to return as often as you like. Each time you return, there is greater joy and reward awaiting you. So relax and visit often! Enchantment awaits…

Concluding Thoughts:

Having birthed *The Enchanted Journey*, it is my wish, as is every mother's, that it will continue to mature into an instrument of love and healing, whose music can be heard throughout the universe.

I would like to quote Erma Bombeck as her sentiments regarding her life and work, mirror my own:

I always had a dream that when I am asked to give an accounting of my life to a higher court, it will go like this: 'So, empty your pockets. What have you got left of your life? Any dreams that were unfulfilled? Any unused talent that we gave you when you were born that you still have left? Any unsaid compliments or bits of love that you haven't spread around?' And I will answer, 'I've nothing to return. I spent everything you gave me. I'm as naked as the day I was born.'

(not) The End.

Just The Beginning...

List of Stories

Order of Endnotes

1 Selye
2 Lazarus & Launier
3 Kabat-Zinn
4 Friedman
5 Williams
6 Shealy
7 Perls
8 Klein & Taylor
9 Rechtshaffen
10 Jung
11 Wilbur
12 Nunley
13 Chopra
14 Pearlin & Schooler
15 James & Nahl
16 Carlson
17 Maslow
18 Eastman & Rozen
19 Mogel
20 Alberto & Troutman
21 Gardner
22 Hanh
23 Morgenstern
24 Rice
25 Dyer
26 Underhill
27 Vasquez
28 Gawain
29 Kübler-Ross
30 Simonton
31 Holmes & Rahe
32 Kobassa
33 Northrup
34 Bach
35 Cameron
36 Goldberg
37 Lamott
38 Ganim & Fox
39 Frank
40 Ackerman
41 Montagu
42 Moore
43 Assagioli
44 Lowell
45 Aslett
46 Collins
47 Ward
48 Thoreau
49 Emerson
50 Weil
51 Bombeck
52 Berk
53 Goodman
54 Adams
55 Siegel

[56] Williams

[57] Graham-Pole

[58] Cousins

[59] Leno

[60] Engelbreit

[61] Hay

[62] Dacher

[63] Zeer

[64] Roth

[65] Hurd & Cassidy

[66] Hirsch

[67] Kjelson

[68] Kahlo

[69] Edwards

[70] Steiner

[71] Baldwin

[72] Roberts

[73] Jacobson

[74] Schultz

[75] Brosse

[76] Wenger, Bagchi, Anand

[77] Wolpe

[78] Maharishi Mahesh Yogi

[79] Carrington

[80] Benson

[81] Matusiak

[82] Rumi

[83] Fredrickson, Cohn, Coffey, Pek and Finkel

References

Ackerman, D. (1990). *A Natural History of the Senses*. New York, NY: A Division of Random House, Inc.

Adams, P. (1994). Love, Humor and Healing. *Good Medicine*, 39, 32.

Alberto, P., & Troutman, A.C. (1998). *Applied Behavior Analysis for Teachers, Fifth Edition*. Paramus, NJ: Prentice-Hall.

Aslett, D. (1981). *Is There Life After Housework? A Revolutionary Approach That Will Free You From the Drudgery of Housework*. Cincinnati, OH: Writer's Digest Books.

Assagioli, R. (1999). *The Act of Will: A Guide to Self-Actualization and Self Realization*. England: David Platts Publishing Co.

Bach, R. (1977). *Illusions: The Adventures of a Reluctant Messiah*. New York, NY: Dell.

Baldwin, R. (1989). You Are Your Child's First Teacher. Berkeley, CA: Celestial Arts

Benson, H. (with Klipper, M.Z.). (1975) In *The Relaxation Response*. New York, NY: Avon Books, Inc.

Berk, L. (1997). Psychoneuroimmunology of Laughter: An Interview with Lee Berk, Dr. PH. *Journal of Nursing Jocularity*, Fall, 7 (3), 46-47.

Bombeck, E: The Estate of. (1996). *Forever Erma*. Kansas City, MO: A Universal Press Syndicate Company.

Brosse, T. "A Psychophysiological Study." *Main Currents in Modern Thought* 4 (1946): 77-84.

Cameron, J. (1996). *The Vein of Gold, A Journey to Your Creative Heart*. New York, NY: Penguin Putnam Inc.

Cameron, J. (with Bryan, M.). (1992). *The Artist's Way, A Spiritual Path to Higher Creativity: A Course in Discovering and Recovering Your Creative Self*. New York, NY: G.P. Putnam's Sons.

Carlson, R. (1997). *Don't Sweat the Small Stuff...and it's all small stuff*. New York, NY: Hyperion.

Carrington, P. (1998). *The Book of Meditation: The Complete Guide to Modern Meditation*. Boston, MA: Element Books Ltd.

Chopra, D. (1989). *Quantam Healing: Exploring the Frontiers of Mind/Body Medicine*. New York, NY: Bantam Books.

Chopra, D. (1994). *The Seven Spiritual Laws of Success, a Practical Guide to The Fulfillment of Your Dreams*. San Rafael, CA: Co-Published by Amber-Allen Publishing, New World Library.

Chopra, D. (1997a). *The Seven Spiritual Laws for Parents: Guiding your Children to Success and Fulfillment*. San Rafael, CA: Harmony Books.

Collins, T.K. (1996). *The Western Guide to Feng Shui: Creating Balance, Harmony, and Prosperity in Your Environment*. Carlsbad, CA: Hay House, Inc.

Corey, G. (1982). *Theory and Practice of Counseling and Psychotherapy, second edition*. Monterey, CA: Brooks/Cole Publishing Company.

Cousins, N. (1985). *Anatomy of an Illness*. New York, NY: Bantam Books.

Dacher, E.S. (1991). *PNI: Psychoneuroimmunology, The New Mind/Body Healing Program*. New York, NY: Paragon House.

Dyer, W. W. (1998). *Wisdom of the Ages: A Modern Master Brings Eternal Truths into Everyday Life.* New York, NY: HarperCollings.

Eastman, M. & Rozen, S.C. (1994). *Taming the Dragon in Your Child: Solutions for Breaking the Cycle of Family Anger.* New York, NY: John Wiley & Sons, Inc.

Edwards, B. (1989). *Drawing On the Right Side of the Brain.* New York, NY: Penguin Putnam.

Emerson, R.W., (2003). *Nature and Selected Essays.* New York, NY: Penguin Group (USA).

Emerson, R.W., as cited in Thoreau (1989).

Engelbreit, M. (2006). *Artful Words: Mary Engelbreit and the Illustrated Quote.* Kansas City, MO: Andrews McMeel Publishing.

Frank, A. (1967). *Anne Frank: The Diary of a Young Girl.* New York, NY: Doubleday.

Fredrickson, B., Cohn, Coffey, K.A., Pek, J. & Finkel, S.M. (2008) Open Hearts Build Lives: Positive Emotions, Induced Through Loving-Kindness Meditation, Build Consequential Personal Resources. *Journal of Personality and Social Psychology.* Vol. 95, No. 5, 1045-1062.

Friedman, M., & Williams, R., as cited in Kabat-Zinn, (1990, p.211).

Ganim, B. (1995). The Power of Art to Heal. *Body, Mind, Spirit,* April/May, 35-38.

Ganim, B. & Fox, S. (1999). *Visual Journaling: Going Deeper Than Words.* Wheaton, IL: The Theosophical Publishing House.

Gardner, H. (1983). *Frames of Mind: The Theory of Multiple Intelligences.* New York, NY: Basic Books.

Gawain, S. (1978). *Creative Visualization.* San Rafael, CA: New World Library.

Goldberg, N. (1986). *Writing Down the Bones—Freeing the Writer Within.* Boston, MA: Shambhala Publications.

Graham-Pole, J. (2000*). Illness and the Art of Creative Self-Expression: Stories and Exercises from the Arts for those with Chronic Illness.* Oakland, CA: New Harbinger Publications.

Hay, L. (1984). *You Can Heal Your Life.* Santa Monica, CA: Hay House.

Hirsch, G. Y. (2008). Gilah Hirsch: Artist, Paint Thyself. *Dateline Dominguez Hills, News for the CSU Comingues Hills Community,* April 24, 2008, 1.

Hirsch, G. Y., as cited in Ganim, (1995, p. 35).

Holmes, T.H., & Rahe, R.H., (1967). The social readjustment rating scale. *Journal of Psychosomatic Research,* 11, 213-18.

Hurd, T. & Cassidy, J. (1992). *Watercolor for the Artistically Undiscovered.* Palo Alto, CA: Klutz Press.

Jacobson, E. as cited in Rice, (1987).

James, L. & Nahl, D. (2000). *Road Rage & Aggressive Driving: Steering Clear of Highway Warfare.* Amherst, NY: Prometheus Books.

Jung, C., as cited in Corey, (1977 p. 33-35).

Kabat-Zinn, J. (1990). *Full Catastrophe Living: Using the Wisdom of Your Body and Mind to Face Stress, Pain and Illness.* New York, NY: Delta.

Kettenmann, A. (1992). *Frida Kahlo 1907-1954: Pain and Passion.* Germany: Taschen.

Kjelson, B. (2001). Art and Healing. *University of Miami Arts and Sciences*, Summer, 18.

Klein, L.C., Taylor, S. E., Lewis, B. P., Gruenewald, T. L., Gurung, R.A.R., & Updegraff, J. A. *Female Responses to Stress: Tend and Befriend, Not Fight or Flight,* Psychological Review, 107(3), 41-429.

Kobassa, S.C. (1979). Stressful life events, personality and health: An Inquiry into hardiness. *Journal of Personality and Social Psychology*, 37, 1-11.

Kübler-Ross, E. (1970). *On Death and Dying.* New York, NY: Macmillan Company.

Lamott, A. (1994). *Bird by Bird.* New York, NY: Anchor Books.

Lazarus, R.S., & Launier, R. (1978). Stress-related transactions between person and environment. In L.A. Pervin & M. Lewis (Eds.), *Perspectives in Interactional Psychology.* New York, NY: Plenum Press.

Leno, J. (1996). *Leading With My Chin.* New York, NY: HarperCollins.

Lowell, C. (2000). *Christopher Lowell's Seven Layers of Design.* New York, NY: Discovery Communications, Inc.

Maharishi Mahesh Yogi, as cited in Throll, (1982).

Maslow, A. H. (1970). *Motivation and Personality.* New York, NY: Harper.

Mogel, W. (2001). *The Blessing of a Skinned Knee.* New York, NY: Penguin Compass.

Monaghan, P., & Viereck, E. (1999). *Meditation: The Complete Guide.* San Rafael, CA: New World Library.

Montagu, A. (1978). *Touching: The Human Significance of the Skin.* New York, NY: Harper & Row.

Moore, T. (1992). *Care of the Soul, A Guide for Cultivating Depth and Sacredness in Everyday Life.* New York, NY: HarperPerennial.

Moore, T. (1994). *The Re-Enchantment of Everyday Life.* New York, NY: HarperCollins.

Morgenstern, J. (1998). *Organizing From the Inside Out: The Foolproof System for Organizing Your Home, Your Office, and Your Life.* New York, NY: Henry   Holt and Company, LLC.

Nhat Hanh, T. (1998). *The Heart of the Buddha's Teaching: Transforming Suffering into Peace, Joy, and Liberation.* Berkeley, CA: Parallax Press.

Northrup, C. (2001). *The Wisdom of Menopause.* New York, NY: Bantam Books.

Nunley, A.P. (1995). *The Symbolic Visualization Process.* Presented at the Inner Counselor Seminar, The Sonrisa Center, McLouth, KS.

Pearlin, L.I. & Schooler, C. (1978). The Structure of Coping. *Journal of Health and Social Behavior,* 19, 2-21.

Perls, F. (1969). *Gestalt Therapy Verbatim.* Moab, UT: Real People Press.

Perls, F. (1973). *The Gestalt Approach and Eye Witness to Therapy.* New York, NY: Bantam.

Rechtshaffen, S. (1996). *Timeshifting: Creating More Time to Enjoy Your Life.* New York, NY: Doubleday.

Rice, P.L. (1987). *Stress and Health: Principles and Practice for Coping and Wellness.* Pacific   Grove, CA: Brooks/Cole Publishing Co.

Roberts, J. (1972). *Seth Speaks.* Englewood Cliffs, New Jersey: Prentice-Hall, Inc.

Roth, G. (1999). *Sweat Your Prayers: Movement as a Spiritual Practice. The Five Rhythms of the Soul.* United States, Penguin.

Roth, G. & Loudon, J. (1998). Maps to Ecstasy: *A Healing Journey for the Untamed Spirit.* San Rafael, CA: New World Library.

Rumi, M.J., as cited in Monaghan & Viereck, (1999).

Schultz, J., & Luthe, W. (1959). *Autogenic Training: A Psychophysiological Approach to Psychotherapy.* New York, NY: Grune & Stratton.

Selye, H. (1950). *The Physiology and Pathology of Exposure to Stress.* Montreal, Canada: Acta.

Selye, H. (1974). *Stress Without Distress.* New York, NY: Lippincott.

Selye, H. (1976). *The Stress of Life, revised edition.* New York, NY: McGraw-Hill.

Shealy, C. N. (1993). *The Self-Healing Workbook: Your Personal Plan for Stress Free Living.* Boston, MA: Element.

Siegel,B. (1986). *Love, Medicine and Miracles.* New York, NY: Harper & Row.

Siegel, B. (1989). *Peace, Love and Healing.* New York, NY: Harper & Row.

Simonton, O.C. (2001). *The Ten Tenets of The Simonton Cancer Program.* Retrieved July 8, 2001, from *http://www.simononcenter.com/Pages/tenents.htm*

Simonton, O.C. & Simonton, S. (1975). Belief systems and management of the emotional aspects of malignancy. *Journal of Transpersonal Psychology,* 7, 29-48.

Spielberger, C.D. (1983). *Manual for the State-Trait Anxiety Inventory for Adults, Form Y.* Redwood City, CA: Mind Garden, Inc.

Spielberger, C.D., Gorsuch, R.L., & Lushene, R.E. (1970). *Manual for the State-Trait Anxiety Inventory (Self-Evaluation Questionnaire).* Palo Alto, CA: Consulting Psychologists Press.

Steiner, R. (1963). *The Life, Nature and Cultivation of Anthroposophy.* London, England: Rudolf Steiner Press.

Thoreau, H.D. (1989). *Walden and Other Writings.* New York, NY: Bantam Books.

Thoreau, H.D., as cited in Cameron, (1992, p. 38).

Throll, D.A., (1982). Transcendental Meditation and Progressive Relaxation: Their Physiological Effects. *Journal of Clinical Psychology,* 38, 522-530.

Underhill, E. (1976). *The Spiritual Life.* New York, NY: Harper & Row.

Vasquez, S. (1985). *Confluent Somatic Therapy.* Presented at the Confluent Somatic Therapy Seminar, Los Angeles, CA.

Ward, L. (1998). *Use What You Have Decorating.* New York, NY: G.P. Putnam's Sons.

Weil, A. (1995). *Spontaneous Healing: Dr. Weil's 8-Week Plan for Optimal Healing Power.* New York, NY: Alfred A. Knopf, Inc.

Weil, A. (1998b). Tai chi lowers blood pressure. *Dr. Andrew Weil's Self Healing, Creating Natural Health for Your Body and Mind,* June, 5.

Weinstein, M. & Goodman, J. (1980). *Everybody's Guide to Noncompetitive Play: Playfair.* San Luis Obispo, CA: Impact Publishers.

Wenger, M.A., & Bagchi, B.K. (1961) Studies of autonomic function in practitioners of yoga in India. Behavioral Science, 6, 312-323.

Wilber, K. (2000). *A Brief History of Everything, revised edition.* Boston, MA:
    Shambhala Publications, Inc.

Wolpe, J. (1958). *Psychotherapy by Reciprocal Inhibition.* Stanford, CA: Stanford University Press.

Zeer, D. (2000). *Office Yoga: Simple Stretches for Busy People.* San Francisco, CA: Chronicle.

LaVergne, TN USA
24 January 2011
213785LV00002B/12/P